T0383482

interesting BIRD NESTS & EGGS

Douglas G. D. Russell

Published by the Natural History Museum, London

This book is dedicated to the diligent, often dangerous, work of the thousands of curators, naturalists, explorers and ornithologists who, over the course of several centuries, have brought back the collections which underpin much of our knowledge of birds, and to my parents, Jean and Gerald Russell, whom I know would be proud.

The Museum

London's Natural History Museum is not only a tourist attraction, but also a world-class research institution that employs over 300 scientists and houses many of the world's most important taxonomic collections. The Museum's bird collection is one of the most comprehensive and significant globally and represents the last three centuries of our quest to understand the avian world. The specimens are key to the ongoing cataloguing of global bird species and subspecies, and underpin our understanding of bird evolution, their anatomy and ecology. Most importantly they are an irreplaceable archive of data crucial to conservation and understanding the effect of anthropogenic climate change.

The author

Douglas G. D. Russell is the Senior Curator at the Natural History Museum, London responsible for the avian egg and nest collections. After studying at Edinburgh Napier University, Douglas started his curatorial career at the National Museum of Scotland, followed by leading public engagement in taxonomy at the Natural History Museum and curatorial work at Scarborough Museums and Galleries. For the last twenty-one years Douglas has overseen the egg and nest collection as part of a team of bird curators at the Natural History Museum Tring.

Acknowledgements

Specimens are all from the Natural History Museum Tring bird collection. I am indebted to my colleagues in the Bird Group and library, especially Dr Robert Prys-Jones, whose mentorship, encouragement, and boundless knowledge has consistently guided me. I am hugely grateful for the care, enthusiasm, and expertise that Jonathan Jackson brought to this project as photographer, and likewise the Publishing team.

MUS.
BRIT.

Humming Bird
Rio de Janiero
Collected by Capt. Cook 1st Voyage

Introduction

The nests and eggs of birds have fascinated us for hundreds of years. At its simplest the nest is any structure made by a bird in which eggs are laid and incubated. Yet the truth is more complicated. Nests protect eggs and young from the elements, thwart predators and help maintain the optimal environment. Ultimately, they allow birds to breed successfully in otherwise challenging environments. From an evolutionary perspective, what seemingly began with a simple scrape on the ground, slowly led to the development of elevated platforms and nesting in natural hollows. Later still, birds learnt to dig out their own cavities, build domed nests and ultimately build what many see as the stereotypical 'nest' – an elevated, purpose-built, multi-layered 'cup-shaped' structure.

In the *Architecture of Birds* (1831), the eminent Scottish naturalist James Rennie (1787–1867) wrote: 'We devote this volume to an examination of birds, in the exercise of their mechanical arts of constructing Nests. This work is the business of their lives – the duty which calls forth that wonderful ingenuity, which no experience can teach, and which no human skill can rival. The infinite variety of modes in which the nests of birds are constructed, and the exquisite adaption of the nest to the peculiar habits of the individual, offer a subject of almost exhaustless interest...'

The earliest surviving nest in the Museum collection belongs to a Glittering-bellied Emerald, *Chlorostilbon lucidus,* collected in November 1768.

Two centuries later our interest in nests continues to grow, energized by field studies supported by laboratory investigations. In the wild, it is hard to determine if birds are choosing specific things to camouflage their nests, or simply using locally available materials. Recent research on captive-bred zebra finches, at the University of St. Andrews, provided the first experimental evidence that birds do make specific choices camouflaging their nests. When offered different coloured strips of otherwise identical paper, the birds routinely chose complimentary colours that matched the paper covering their nest box and walls of their enclosure. If the walls of the nest box and enclosure were pink they chose pink strips to build their nests. If the walls were blue, they chose blue. Such novel research is helping revolutionize our understanding of birds. Yet the basic breeding biology of only 30 per cent of bird species globally is well known. This paucity of knowledge is particularly challenging in the tropical regions, where the breeding ecology of around 80 per cent of bird species is barely known as their nests have rarely or never been found. For instance, the breeding ecology of the Long-crested Pygmy-Tyrant *Lophotriccus eulophotes*, a small flycatcher of the western Amazonian forests, is completely undocumented.

Museums continue to serve a critical and unique role as the principal archivists of newly-discovered specimens. In 2023 the Natural History Museum, London, working in partnership with local people, ornithologists and BirdLife International in the Democratic Republic of São Tomé and Príncipe, helped preserve and research the first known nest of the Critically Endangered Sao Tome Grosbeak, *Crithagra concolor*.

This is a book about bird nests and eggs held in the ornithological collection of the Natural History Museum Tring. It is not a field guide to nests in the wild. All the nests and eggs shown are preserved historical examples from the Museum's research collection. The earliest surviving nest in the collection belongs to a Glittering-bellied Emerald, *Chlorostilbon lucidus* (see p.4). This small, innocuous, typical hummingbird nest was collected in November 1768 in Rio de Janeiro during the first voyage of Captain James Cook on HMS *Endeavour*.

The Museum is gradually digitizing more than 5,000 historical bird nests – all with important information. For example, the nest and eggs of the Southern Fiscal, *Lanius collaris*, a medium sized black-and-white shrike from South Africa, were collected at Leeuspruit, South Africa on 10th August 1902 (see p.8). The label showing the exact date and locality is critical as the more data we hold as to the identity of the species, and when, where and who collected it, the better. Firstly, we can be more confident the nest builder was accurately identified and, secondly, it allows us to study and compare nests and eggs temporally and geographically.

A typical Southern Fiscal nest is a bulky, very thick-walled cup built solely for the short-lived purpose of incubating the eggs and raising the young until they fledge several weeks later. What does this fragile, seemingly inconsequential, nest have to tell us so long after it was meant to gently pass from existence? Firstly, it tells us basic ecological data about the species that built it and, secondly, it gives us a voucher specimen that serves as a verifiable and permanent record of how this specific nest, at this time and place, was built and what materials were used. It inadvertently captures a little of the early 20th century environment of South Africa. Advances in molecular biology have enabled greater analysis of historical bird nests in museum collections. They are a rich yet vastly underutilized source of genetic information, which could answer a range of ecological and evolutionary questions. This nest is an encapsulated time-capsule of a past environment, from which the flora and fauna of a habitat might be reconstructed using DNA extracted from the plants and any animal remains identified within the nest. If you look carefully, you can see fragments of woven cloth and string have been built into the nest. This behaviour was not new to the early 1900s – shrikes are well-known to use a wide variety of materials found locally, including man-made materials like

Nest and eggs (below) of the Southern Fiscal, *Lanius collaris*, a medium-sized black-and-white shrike from South Africa with detail of woven fragments (opposite).

string, rags, and, more recently, plastic, in their nests. What this nest so succinctly and effectively illustrates is that it is not the bird's behaviour that has changed, it is the nature and longevity of our rubbish. The earliest account of birds incorporating discarded rubbish into their nests was written by the Reverand John Lightfoot (1735–1788) in 1785. Whilst describing nests of the Common Reed Warbler, *Acrocephalus scirpaceus,* he noted that string had clearly been added to the nest by the birds: 'The nest is tied on to the reeds with dead grass, and sometimes (as being more eligible when it can be had) even with thread and packthread, emulating the work of a seamstress as was the case of the nest exhibited in the drawing.'

In 2019 one global review of *c.* 11,000 bird nests found that 31 per cent included human produced debris. Worldwide, millions of tons of our waste are discarded every day. Some of this rubbish, for example plastic string, is picked up by birds and incorporated into their nests. Birds might choose polypropylene rope because it is strong – just like we do – or white plastic as a decoration to signal to a mate. Birds

have even been found to incorporate cigarette butts into their nests, a behaviour which has the benefit of acting as a parasite repellent alongside all the toxicity that also threatens their human smokers.

We are in a transition period as climate change, biodiversity loss, habitat destruction, pollution and deforestation are relentlessly driven by unsustainable human behaviour. If nests are, as research has suggested, a cultural tradition in which the choice of nest materials is learned as well as innate, what will the nests of tomorrow be constructed from if we do not curb our enthusiasm for throwaway culture?

Note on taxonomic arrangement

The taxonomic arrangement and scientific names follow *The Howard and Moore Complete Checklist of the Birds of the World*, 4th edn., vol. 1: *Non-passerines and vol. 2: Passerines* by Edward C. Dickinson, James V. Remsen Jr. and Leslie Christidis.

Subspecies are discrete, diagnosable populations within a species. Where possible, the subspecies that built the nest, or the egg(s) illustrated, is quoted underneath the common name. For example, the Syrian Ostrich, *Struthio camelus syriacus*, is a subspecies of the Common Ostrich, *Struthio camelus*.

A late 18th century artwork depicting discarded rubbish incorporated into the nest of a Common Reed Warbler, *Acrocephalus scirpaceus,* found on 26th July 1783 and figured in *Philosophical Transactions of the Royal Society of London*.

Struthio camelus syriacus Rothsch.

This egg was taken by
Charles Doughty from a
nest at BISEITA, within
10 miles of Lat. 30 N. and
Long. 38 E. 1 about 1880.
Given by Doughty to Colonel
Lawrence who gave it to
me in 1922.   R. Meinertzhagen.

1941.4.1.69   I

Syrian Ostrich

Struthio camelus syriacus

The largest, fastest running and heaviest of the flightless birds, ostriches were, in the past, found across Africa and parts of the Middle East; now they are only found naturally in Africa. The extinct Syrian Ostrich, a subspecies of the Common Ostrich, was historically found in the deserts of Syria and Arabia. Ostriches do not build nests. Instead, the male makes a shallow scrape around 3 m (10 ft) in diameter in the sand or soil. They nest as a pair or as a group, including a territorial male, with a major female and secondary females. Only a handful of eggs and specimens of the Syrian Ostrich remain in museums, and almost everything known about these birds has been gleaned from these and historical reports. This egg was collected by the explorer Charles Doughty in northern Saudi Arabia and gifted to T. E. Lawrence (1888–1935) 'Lawrence of Arabia', who in turn gave it to Colonel Richard Meinertzhagen (1878–1967) and thence to Lord Walter Rothschild (1868–1937). An account of their breeding suggests that they laid between 12 to 21 eggs in the winter, usually at the foot of an isolated hill, close together, half-buried in sand to protect them from sudden rain, and with a surrounding narrow trench to allow water to run off. Ostrich hunting on horseback in Arabia was common and the eggs were considered a delicacy, with the shells used for decoration, but the import of rifles to Arabia during the First World War increased the efficacy of hunting, and extinction followed swiftly in the mid-20th century.

Average size of egg: 142.8 x 115.8 mm (5½ x 4½ in)
Clutch size: 5–11
Collected: *c.* 1880 Biseita Plain, Saudi Arabia
by Charles Doughty (1843–1926)
Conservation Status: Extinct

Dwarf Cassowary

Casuarius bennetti

Cassowaries are the biggest native forest birds of northeastern Australia and New Guinea, and all species are flightless. The Dwarf Cassowary is found across the mountains and lowlands of east New Guinea, as well as New Britain, the largest island in the Bismarck Archipelago, off the northeastern coast of New Guinea, where they were probably introduced. Like ostriches, the Dwarf Cassowary doesn't make a nest as such but rather a shallow depression between the buttress roots of large trees, which it sparsely lines with leaves and other material. This Dwarf Cassowary egg is the oldest known to science and the first to be described of the species. The Indigenous people of New Britain, from whom the egg and adult birds were acquired in 1857, called it the 'Mooruk'. The egg was acquired by the Rev. Dr George Alexander Turner (1818–1891) and subsequently sent on to London and presented to the British Museum in 1858. How the cassowaries might have reached New Britain, especially as New Britain like many oceanic islands has far fewer bird species than the mainland, has long been debated. That this egg and adults were purchased in New Britain is interesting. There were long-established trading networks involving cassowaries and their products, such as elaborately carved cassowary bone daggers, around the Vitiaz Strait between New Britain and Papua New Guinea. This trading network was formerly extensive but declined after the German administration in 1884, so it is likely the cassowaries were introduced to New Britain several times over the centuries.

Average size of egg: 137.2 x 89.5 mm (5.4 x 3.5 in)
Clutch size: 3–5
Collected: New Britain, 1857
Conservation Status: Least Concern

Emperor Goose

Anser canagicus

The Emperor Goose is a medium-sized, stocky Arctic goose with beautiful grey plumage delicately barred with black and white. It winters in the ice-free coasts of the Aleutians, Canada and Alaska Peninsula and migrates north in the spring to breed in eastern Siberia and the Bering Sea coast of mainland Alaska, a migration timed to coincide with the melting of the ice and snow, which determines the availability of food and nest sites. The female digs several scrapes before settling on one to build her nest. She drags dead vegetation into the nest after her first egg is laid, and adds more vegetation and a covering of down feathers for insulation after each subsequent egg is laid. Subsistence hunting in Alaska and coastal oil pollution threaten the numbers of Emperor Goose together with climate change, which is the major threat to many species dependent on tundra habitat for breeding. Computer modelling suggests that 54 per cent of the habitat for this species could be lost by 2070.

Nest size: width 350 mm (13¾ in); depth 60 mm (2¼ in)
Clutch size: 3–5
Collected: 20 June 1910, Quinhagak nr. Arolik River, Goodnews Bay, southwest Alaska
Conservation status: Near Threatened

Green-winged Teal

Anas crecca

Many of the 174 waterfowl species nest on the ground near water, but a few species choose to nest in holes or in tree nests built by other species. This nest, made by the Green-winged Teal, is typical of most ground-nesting ducks. After selecting a site near to water in a suitable habitat, the female teal scrapes out a bowl with her feet and lays the first of her eight or so eggs in the bowl, gently pulling in surrounding vegetation. Only once the final egg is laid does she insulate the nest with her down feathers and commence incubation.

Box size: width 230 mm (9 in); height 90 mm (3½ in)
Clutch size: 6-9
Collected: 12 May 1905, St Helens, Isle of Wight
Conservation status: Least Concern

Common Pheasant

Phasianus colchicus colchicus

Pheasant species can show a range of breeding strategies but most are polygynous, meaning one male mates with and defends several females in a 'harem' but each female only mates with the single male. All pheasant species nest on the ground, usually in a shallow depression that can be lined with sparse vegetation, and the nest is often hidden under a bush or overhang. Comon Pheasants originated in Asia but are now one of the most introduced and intensively studied species globally. They were first introduced into Europe from Asia over 1,600 years ago during the Roman occupation, and a pattern of successive introductions has been repeated since the 11th century. They are now one of the most widespread and abundant non-native birds in Britain and a common sight in farmland and woodland habitats. This nest is a typical example of a Common Pheasant nest. The female selects the nest site, usually close to her wintering range, ensuring it is at a distance from the other females in the harem and in a secluded location in tall vegetation. Pheasants simply grab what they can from the scrape and toss it back towards their body; this nest includes straw and loose breast feathers from the female. Nests can be lined with grasses, leaves or fine twigs, basically anything within easy distance of the nest, but many are unlined. The female alone incubates the eggs.

Box size: width 230 mm (9 in); cup depth 80 mm (3 in)
Clutch size: 7–15
Collected: late 1800s or early 1900s
Conservation status: Least Concern

Little Grebe

Tachybaptus ruficollis ruficollis

Grebes have, perhaps unfairly, been referred to as 'efficient if not very elaborate nest builders'. Males and females build the nest, but the male does most of the work. The birds dive for sodden, often decaying, aquatic plants around the nest site – they can bring up as many as 100 beak loads in 50 minutes – and use this material to build a floating platform, which is securely anchored to waterside vegetation. They eventually build up a sufficient mass of material to climb on to and shape into a flat cone. Once the nest is finished, copulation and egg laying follows. Sometimes fresh plant material is added to the nest and it has been suggested this may aid fermentation, which helps provide warmth during incubation.

Box size: width 300 mm (11¾ in); height 125 mm (5 in)
Clutch size: 3–5
Collected: nest – late 1800s or early 1900s, unknown provenance probably Isle of Wight, UK by Jeremiah M. Goodall (1862-1939); eggs – 10 June 1915, Littlecote, Wiltshire
Conservation status: Least Concern

in tree of *Eugenia*
ratiflora 4-5 m above
ground at 250-300 m
elevation in woodland
② - egg found under
tree is # ①

1/2016.3.1
Ptilinopus dupetithouarsii
Mohotani, Marquesas
17 April 1975.

Found on ground under
nest; nest in tree of
Eugenia ratiflora 4-5 m
above ground at 250-300 m
elevation in woodland
① nest is # ②

White-capped Fruit-Dove

Ptilinopus dupetithouarsii dupetithouarsii

The fifty-seven fruit-dove species are all found in Southeast Asia and Oceania, with White-capped Fruit-Doves only found on seven of the 15 isolated Marquesas Islands of French Polynesia in the southern Pacific Ocean. This small group of islands is one of the remotest archipelagos in the world, the nearest land being Tahiti some 1,368 km (850 miles) to the southwest. Like many small islands, a large proportion of the vegetation of this island has been damaged by the introduction of sheep and goats in the 19th century and, whilst the White-capped Fruit-Dove is currently considered Least Concern, the continued degradation and destruction of suitable habitat could be a major threat in the future. The establishment of the Motane Nature Reserve in 1992 was the first positive step in protecting this group of islands and its endemic colourful, frugivorous doves. This nest, a simple, loose platform nest of sticks and other vegetation, is typical of all pigeons and doves. But, unlike most pigeons and doves, the White-capped Fruit-Dove only lays a single, pure white egg.

Overall nest platform: width 190 mm (7 ½ in); depth 50 (2 in)
Clutch size: 1
Collected: 17 April 1975, uninhabited volcanic island of Mohotani (Montane) in a Beach Cherry tree, *Eugenia reinwardtiana,* by Jean-Claude Thibault
Conservation status: Least Concern

Sunbittern

Eurypyga helias helias

The Sunbittern is a strange, heron-like bird of forest streams and marshes in the Neotropics. It is the only member of its family, and this ancient bird has a sibling evolutionary relationship with the flightless and endangered Kagu of New Caledonia in the southwest Pacific Ocean. Together they are the sole members of the Eurypygiformes, an order which can be traced back 60 million years. Their biogeography is puzzling – the relatively plain, silver-grey Kagu lays a single egg in a scrape nest in the leaf litter, whereas the spectacularly colourful Sunbittern, lays up to three eggs in a shallow, open, saucer-shaped nest of mud reinforced with grasses and leaves built on the horizontal branches of trees. This difference in nesting led to confusion when the Zoological Society of London first attempted to breed them in captivity. In May 1865, the staff noticed their Sunbitterns were carrying twigs and grasses around and unsuccessfully trying to mix wet dirt with moss. Their breeding in the wild was largely unknown but this observation led to the inspired decision to supply the captive birds with copious amounts of wet clay, mud and straw. The birds rapidly constructed a flat, mud nest on a pole about 3 metres (10 feet) from the ground and that summer the birds successfully bred in captivity for the first time.

Nest size: 165 x 112 x 45 mm (6.4 x 4.4 x 1.7 in)
Clutch size: 2–3
Collected: 1895, from a tree in Ilha das Onças, Pará, Brazil by Émil August Goeldi (1859–1917)
Conservation status: Least Concern

Eurypyga helias helias N/139.1
Isla das Oncas, Pará
Brazil.
Emil August Goeldi

L

1952.8.27
555

Gould's Frogmouth

Batrachostomus stellatus

Frogmouths, or podargids, are aptly named for their large, flattened bills and wide, gaping mouths. The nests of all podargids are simple but rather beautiful platform structures. The three *Podargus* and one *Rigidipenna* species are restricted to Australia, New Guinea and the Solomon Islands and all build stick nests with a simple cup. The twelve *Batrachostomus* species in Asia have smaller cup nests of bark, down, spiders' webs and lichen, built on a horizontal branch. Relatively little is known about the breeding biology of Asian frogmouths and few nests of Gould's Frogmouth have been described. This nest is a typically neat, felted pad with a tiny shallow depression. At only 5 cm (2 in) across it is perhaps surprisingly small given the 25 cm (10 in) long adult that constructed it, but it is more than sufficient to carry the single egg the female lays. This example is one of the very few nests known to science. It contained one young, which had fledged and flown from the nest three days previously and was sitting perched with an adult about 18 m (20 yd) away on the day the nest was collected.

Nest pad: 50 mm (2 in) wide
Clutch size: 1
Collected: 16th March 2003, Khao Nor Chu Chi in the forests of Krabi Province, southern Thailand by Peter R. Colston
Conservation status: Near Threatened

Sri Lanka Frogmouth

Batrachostomus moniliger

These cryptically coloured nocturnal birds are notoriously difficult to study, and the work undertaken by Thomas Reid Davys Bell (1863-1948), who collected these specimens, helped show the distribution and breeding dates of these birds in Karnataka State in southwestern India and the fascinating composition of their small platform nests. Each nest is constructed by both sexes and placed on a horizonal branch or fork 2–6 m (6½–19½ ft) above the ground. The small, densely packed, circular pad is only 5–6 cm (2–2½ in) across and largely composed of the birds' down feathers bound with cobwebs into which small twigs and leaves have been layered and incorporated. The outside has small leaves and other plant material added to it to provide some camouflage, and the relatively large egg is laid in a small concavity in the centre of the nest.

Nest pad: width 65 mm (2 ½ in); cup depth 10 mm (½ in)
Clutch size: 1
Collected: March 1909, Western Ghats mountains, India
Conservation status: Least Concern

Sabine's Spinetail

Rhaphidura sabini

Spinetail swifts are found throughout Central Africa and use their adhesive saliva to carefully build a nest made of small twigs. Each nest is around 8 cm (3 in) in width and each twig is carefully glued in place to make a small half-cupped nest, which is then securely attached, using the glutinous saliva excreted from under the bird's tongue, to a suitable site amongst large roots, a niche or a hollow in a tree. Two to three eggs are then laid. Unlike some *Aerodramus* swiftlets (see p.34), whose colonies can number in the millions, spinetails tend to nest singly or as two pairs. Sabine's Spinetails are not globally threatened but there is thought to have been a decline in their numbers in Kenya during the 20th century. Ironically their numbers seem to have increased in Liberia, where they have been able to utilize secondary habitats despite increasing forest fragmentation.

Nest size: width 80 mm (3 in); depth 25 mm (1 in)
Clutch size: 2–3
Collected: probably collected by George Latimer Bates (1863–1940) in Southwest Cameroon *c.* 1912
Conservation status: Least Concern

Chaetura sabini
No. 3555   XI.14   W. Africa
221 - 4
(1)   18 X   12.5
(2)   17.5 X   12.5
(3)   17 X   12

Spinetail
e swift.
April 1912.

White-nest Swiftlet

Aerodramus fuciphagus fuciphagus

The opaque 'white' nests of the White-nest Swiftlet are amongst the most unusual in the avian world. For centuries they have been used to flavour the eponymously named 'bird nest soup'. Not famed for its flavour, the soup is used as a traditional medicine with alleged miracle cures, but there is no proven benefit to consuming the nests; however, its appeal is as strong as ever. The nests are made mainly of dried strands of amorphous mucin glycoprotein, secreted by the male swiftlets during the nesting and breeding season from a pair of sublingual glands under the tongue. The birds nest colonially in huge numbers, building their small, self-supporting, bracket-shaped nests in around 39 to 55 days deep within the walls of caves, the most famous being the Niah Caves in Sarawak, Malaysia. The harvesting and exploitation of some swiftlet nests for food has a long history and was first noted in English by the ornithologist John Ray in 1678. The trade in nests was, however, already well-established when the Dutch and British founded trading posts in Banten, northwestern Java in 1603 and this nest was collected as part of that trade in the 1800s. The accompanying label states: 'Class III B. Food Products', showing that it was exhibited to illustrate its importance as a trade product during the 1862 International Exhibition in London.

Nest size: width 60 mm (2¼); depth 30 mm (1 in)
Clutch size: 2
Collected: mid-1800s, islands off 'Junk Ceylon'
now Phuket Island, Thailand
Conservation status: Least Concern

Collocalia nidifica

MUS.
BRIT. Isles adjoining Junk Ceylon

CLASS III.
B. Food Products. BM Nest
Reg N.781-3

Edible Birds-nests (1st sort)
Collocalia nidifica.
Isles adjoining
No. 4158 Junk Ceylon.

Jud

Juan Fernández Firecrown

Sephanoides fernandensis

The Juan Fernández Firecrown is one of the nine species of hummingbird now listed as Critically Endangered. The sexes of this little hummingbird are very different – the male is a lovely cinnamon-orange whilst the female is bluish-green and, because of this, they were previously described as separate species. They are only found on Robinson Crusoe Island, in the Juan Fernández Archipelago, South Pacific Ocean. Compared with other hummingbird species their cup-shaped nests are comparatively large structures. Made from the soft, reddish wood of the *Dicksonia* tree fern and padded out with moss, the nests were found attached to climbing ferns on one side and, at the bottom, to a fine branch or slender climbing rhizome.

Nest size: cup width 20 mm (¾ in); cup depth 25 mm (1 in)
Clutch size: 2
Collected: mid-1800s, Juan Fernández Islands
Conservation status: Critically Endangered

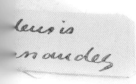

Common Cuckoo

Cuculus canorus canorus

Cuckoos have a wide range of breeding strategies, from cooperative breeding through to the brood-parasitism. The cuckoo family contains more than 50 per cent of all the known brood parasite species but, despite this, the majority (*c.* 60 per cent) largely raise their own young and build their own nests, with a small number being cooperative breeders. The Common Cuckoo is perhaps the most famous obligate brood parasite i.e. a species which relies entirely on other species to raise their young. These open-cup nests are part of a comprehensive series of over 30 nests, built by thirteen different UK hosts, and the Common Cuckoo eggs found in them in the 1860s. More than one hundred bird species across Europe, the Middle East and Asia have been recorded as having Common Cuckoo eggs in their nests, including flycatchers, warblers, buntings, chats and pipits. Female specific lineages, called gentes, have evolved to mimic the eggs of different host species and *c.* 77 per cent of eggs closely match the eggs of the chosen hosts. After the Cuckoo egg has hatched, the chick pushes the other host's eggs or chicks out of the nest with their backs. This leaves the Cuckoo alone in the nest to be fed by its foster parents.

Rock Pipit nest box size: width 120 mm (4 ¾ in); height 75 mm (3 in)
Clutch size: 1 Common Cuckoo egg in Rock Pipit nest
Collected: Rock Pipit nest and eggs – 1869, Faroe Islands; others Churt, Surrey, UK by ornithologist Philip Crowley (1837–1900)
Conservation status: Least Concern

Laysan Rail

Zapornia palmeri

This nest and egg of the extinct Laysan Rail is one of the only examples known to science. The bulky cup nest consists of grass woven together with very fine shreds of leaves, and a little down. It would have been built in grass tussocks where it was concealed, and usually roofed over by vegetation. Nests were placed at the end of cleverly camouflaged tunnels. The small flightless bird was endemic to the northwest Hawaiian island of Laysan and when this nest was obtained in 1891, they were still relatively abundant and reported to be scurrying at mouse-like speed round the island. A combination of intense guano mining and the introduction of rabbits and guinea pigs in 1903 devastated the island's formerly pristine nesting habitat. It is thought that the birds consequently died out on Laysan around 1923. Their extinction was briefly deferred as a small number had been transferred to the Midway Atoll, but the introduction of rats, which then predated on the eggs, chicks and adults, to Midway Atoll in 1943 spelled disaster and the last of the species died in 1944.

Nest size: cup width 70 mm (2¾ in); cup depth 40 mm (1½ in)
Clutch size: 2–3
Collected: 24 June 1891, Laysan, northwestern Hawaiian Islands by ornithologist Henry C. Palmer
Conservation status: Extinct

Emperor Penguin

Aptenodytes forsteri

Whilst mistakenly synonymous with the cold, only two species of penguin, the Emperor and the Adélie, are truly Antarctic, with the Endangered Galápagos Penguin, found off the tropical coast of Ecuador, being the most northerly. Some penguins nest in burrows, rock crevices or build nests of stones, but the Emperor has perhaps the most unusual method – the eggs are incubated directly on the feet of the male. The female lays one egg in May to June amid the Antarctic winter, when the average daily temperature in the coldest regions can be around –60 to –65°C (–51 to –54°F). She then carefully transfers her single egg to the male, who balances it on his feet and incubates it for around 62 to 66 days. During this time the males remain on the sea ice, gathered in large huddles in the darkness, waiting patiently for the females to return from feeding at sea. This egg was collected on Captain Robert Falcon Scott's infamous last expedition to the Antarctic in 1911. It was thought the embryo within the egg would shed light on the evolution of all birds and, whilst this subsequently did not prove to be the case, it remains one of the most iconic, hard won, and extraordinary objects in any museum.

Average size of egg: 119 x 82.3 mm (4 ½ x 3 ¼ in)
Clutch size: 1
Collected: 20 July 1911, Cape Crozier, Ross Island, Antarctica by Apsley Cherry Garrard (1886–1959), Henry 'Birdie' Bowers (1883–1912) and Edward Wilson (1872–1912) of the British Antarctic Expedition, 1910
Conservation status: Near Threatened

1916.9.8.
3.

Brit. Ant. Exped., 1910.

No.
Date
Lat.
Long.
Depth
Air Temp.
Water Temp.
Therm. No:
Instrument

Emperor Penguin By Cmre C. Royds.

Gerrard.

European Storm-Petrel

Hydrobates pelagicus

Most storm-petrels nest in burrows about 10–30 crn (4–12 in) long but can also nest in crevices in rocks or caves. On occasion they dig their own burrows in soft earth, but commonly reuse abandoned burrows made by other animals such as rabbits. The male and female pair for life and often meet at the same burrow year-on-year. If the storm-petrels excavate their own burrow, it will be about 5–8 cm (2–3 in) wide with a slightly larger chamber at the end. This chamber is lined with plant materials such as scraps of grasses, brackens or seaweed (as shown here). It is in this chamber that the female lays her single, comparatively large, egg – its mass is usually 20–30 per cent of her bodyweight. The stronghold for the European Storm-Petrel is still undoubtedly the Faroe Islands, Denmark where 90 per cent (250,000 pairs) of the world population are thought to breed.

Box size: width 200 mm (7 ¾ in); height 90 mm (3 ½ in)
Clutch size: 1
Collected: 11 July 1894, Auskerry Island, Orkney by John Peace
Conservation status: Least Concern

Name *Stormy Petrel*
Locality *Auskerry, Stronsay*
Taken by *John Peace*
Date *11th July 1894*
No. of Eggs in Set. *1* Set Mark
John R. Gunn, Collector.

Northern Gannet

Morus bassanus

Northern Gannets breed in sizable, dense colonies. The largest and most famous of these is undoubtedly the internationally important breeding colony on the Bass Rock, an island in the Firth of Forth in the east of Scotland. Each summer, more than 150,000 Gannets arrive and nest on the flat cliff ledges of this forbidding 106 m (348 ft) high volcanic rock, so many that they make the island look as though it is covered in snow from a distance. Gannets collect nest material communally from the island, the adjacent islands and the sea. The male collects much of the seaweed, grass and other flotsam, which he delivers to the female who draws these assorted materials together by the simple sideways movements of the bill. This pile of nesting materials (opposite) comprises mostly grasses and feathers, and the underlying materials would have been cemented together and to the rock with excreta. What you see here are largely fine materials into which the single egg has been laid. In 2022, the Bass Rock, which supports half the global Northern Gannet population, was severely affected by the Avian Flu pandemic. Globally, it is estimated that this outbreak led to the death of 97 million birds across many species, of which around 3.8 million deaths occurred in the UK.

Nest size: width 250 mm (9 ¾ in); depth 50 mm (2 in)
Clutch size: 1
Collected: 8 May 1911, Bass Rock, Firth of Forth, Scotland by Nathaniel Charles Rothschild (1877–1923)
Conservation status: Least Concern

Pied Avocet

Recurvirostra avosetta

Like other avocets, the Pied Avocet breeds colonially, and each nest is little more than a sparsely-lined scrape in the mud into which three to four camouflaged, clay-coloured eggs, spotted with black, are laid. In the 1700s they were a relatively common sight on the shores of southeast England in summertime, and in the early 1800s, they were still breeding in considerable numbers. But the draining of many English marshes, begun in the 12th century, led to their loss as a British breeding bird by the mid 1800s. War changed their British fortunes. The Second World War necessitated extensive defences of the Suffolk coast that limited disturbance. At the same time, the deliberate flooding of coastal marshes, aimed at detering an enemy landing, inadvertently recreated suitable breeding habitats – seven pairs of avocet were recorded as making their nests at Minismere, Suffolk in 1947, the first UK nests recorded for a century. Since the 1970s they have been one of the most well-known icons of British bird conservation, and you may recognize them as the logo for the UK's Royal Society for the Protection of Birds (RSPB).

Nest size: width 90 mm (3 ½ in); depth 20 mm (¾ in)
Clutch size: 3–4
Collected: May 1980, mouth of the River Seine, France
Conservation status: Least Concern

GOLDEN PLOVER

Nº 304

Golden Plover

Pluvialis apricaria apricaria

Golden Plovers usually share a life-long pair bond and build their nests in flat, openly-vegetated areas like moors. First, the male makes a shallow scrape and, as this example shows, lines it with moss, lichen and other plant materials into which three to four eggs are laid at intervals of 48 to 60 hours. Since this nest of four eggs was found in 1884 there has been a decrease in the birds' range in northwestern Europe, mainly due to habitat changes, such as cultivation and afforestation of their heathland habitat. The major threat facing Golden Plovers is now thought to be climate change. Craneflies and other flies are a key source of food for adult Eurasian Golden Plovers and their chicks, and the timing of their breeding and the emergence of their cranefly prey are synchronized, and both are related to temperature.

Box size: width 150 mm (6 in); height 80 mm (3 in)
Clutch size: 3–4
Collected: 14 April 1884, Haltwhistle, Northumberland
by William Mark Pybus (1851–1924)
Conservation status: Least Concern

Red-necked Phalarope

Phalaropus lobatus

The Red-necked Phalarope is in a family of birds that generally all prefer exposed, wetland breeding habitats. Most are intertidal, shorebird species which, outside the breeding season, feast on the wealth of invertebrates found in mudflats and similar areas. Phalaropes, of which the Red-Necked Phalarope is the most delicate of the three species, are the exception, spending the non-breeding season wintering at sea in the tropics. Six months before this nest was found in Scotland, the birds that built it were almost certainly off the west coast of South America. The nest begins as a scrape a few days before the first egg is laid. Then the male gradually tosses in heather, grass and twigs and continues the process whilst the first three eggs are laid. A letter from the collector, written on 4 July 1899 and placed with the nest, illustrates the rarity of the Red-necked Phalarope in Orkney: 'This is the first I ever found and the only one I have known to be found on mainland of Orkney. So, I trust you will appreciate and be pleased with it.'

Box size: width 220 mm (8 ¾ in); height 95 mm (3 ¾ in)
Clutch size: 4
Collected: 17 June 1899, St Ola, Orkney, Scotland
by John R. Gunn
Conservation status: Least Concern

Great Auk

Pinguinus impennis

Auks, murres and puffins are seabirds that primarily breed colonially, often laying their eggs on bare ground in cavities, crevices and rock ledges, without the addition of nesting materials. (Puffins, murrelets and auklets are the exceptions as they construct nest burrows.) The flightless Great Auks were once widespread from North America to Europe, inhabiting the low Arctic and boreal seas of the North Atlantic. About 70 cm (28 in) tall, they were about the same size and weight as the Magellanic Penguin from the coastal areas of southern Argentina and Chile. Penguins and Great Auks are not closely related but their body shapes are a classic example of convergent evolution, both occupying similar ecological niches with flightlessness and shape optimized for pursuit diving. Evidence shows they coexisted with humans for millennia but flightlessness, colonial breeding and size made their breeding colonies an easy source of food for itinerant sailors and collectors. CT-scans of eggs have helped reconstruct their breeding biology, the shape and eggshell thickness suggesting that the Great Auk incubated in an upright posture on bare rock surfaces, its pyriform-shaped egg providing stability during incubation, and its relatively thick shell at the equator and pointed end providing protection. The infinite variety of patterns found on the few eggs in collections show that, like guillemots, each egg's unique patterning acts as a signature ensuring that, in the dense chaos of a colony, parents could always recognize and care for their own egg.

Average size of egg: 124 x 76 mm (4 ¾ x 3 in)
Clutch size: 1
Collected: *c.* 1760–1780s by Professor Lazzaro Spallanzani (1729-1799), University of Pavia
Conservation status: Extinct

1941
1
2.

NUMBER
THREE

Champley Collection
C. at Rector
Nov 7. 901

Parasitic Jaeger

Stercorarius parasiticus

The Parasitic Jaeger, also known as the Arctic Skua, is one of seven skua and jaeger species found globally. Jaeger is German for 'hunter' – an apt name for these highly efficient oceanic predators. In the UK, the Parasitic Jaeger is only found in northern Scotland, at the southerly limit of its circumpolar range. Arctic Skuas arrive back at their remote Scottish breeding sites around mid-April. This is a typical example of their nest; a small depression has been made in the moss and other nesting material, and sparsely lined with grasses, into which two dull, olive-brown eggs speckled with dark grey and brown are laid. The demographic of birds breeding on the Isle of Noss has changed considerably since this nest was collected in the 1800s. Recent studies have estimated that the population of Arctic Skua in Orkney, Shetland and Handa declined by around 81 per cent between 1992 and 2015. Climate change is driving shifts in sea surface temperatures, and this is thought to be causing a decline in the population of Lesser Sandeels, *Ammodytes marinus*, one of the key food sources of the Arctic Skua and the puffin, kittiwake, Common Guillemot and Arctic Tern – the species that they often steal food from.

Nest size: width 180 mm (7 in); cup depth 40 mm (1½ in)
Clutch size: 2
Collected: June 1897, Isle of Noss, Shetland Islands
Conservation status: Least Concern

RICHARDSON'S SKUA, 2 cl.
Stercorarius crepidatus.
Noss, Shetland. W. Mark Pybus.

STERCORARIUS PARASITICUS
NOSS, SHETLANDS
1 JUNE 1947

Brown Noddy

Anous stolidus stolidus

Brown Noddy are terns found in the tropics. They breed in colonies in a wide variety of tropical locations on rocks, islets and islands up to 4,000 km (2,500 miles) either side of the equator. Like many seabirds they only lay a single egg and, where a nest is built, both sexes contribute to building it, though many lay their eggs directly in a scrape on bare rock. Depending on the nest site, for example on islands with trees, Brown Noddy can construct platform nests of twigs in trees or an agglomeration of shells, coral, twigs and bones, even dead marine animals. This nest example is made largely of guano (seabird excrement) and seems to contain a colony of ctenostomes (a type of bryozoan).

Nest size: width 170 mm (6 ¾ in); depth 70 mm (2 ¾ in)
Clutch size: 1
Collected: 8 November 1921, Saint Peter and Saint Paul Archipelago, central Atlantic during Ernest Shackleton's final expedition by Sir George Hubert Wilkins (1888–1958)
Conservation status: Least Concern

Hen Harrier

Circus cyaneus cyaneus

Once widespread, the Hen Harrier was lost on mainland UK during the 19th century due to hunting and changes in land use. In the mid-1900s, following the introduction in the UK of the Protection of Birds Act 1954, and strengthened by the Wildlife and Countryside Act in 1981, the remaining Hen Harrier population on the Orkney Islands were able to re-colonize at least some of their former range. This nest, containing a clutch of typically white eggs, is built of small sticks and grass by the female, and would have been assembled on the ground, concealed in dense grass or scrub. The name Hen Harrier is a sad testimony to their ongoing persecution as they opportunistically prey upon game bird chicks, alongside the small mammals that tend to make up a major part of their diet. Dramatic changes in land use (in areas like the Ophir Hills on Orkney where this nest was found), of increasing amounts of land set aside for intensive pasture, and subsequent increases in the number of sheep, have severely reduced the amount of unmanaged grassland on which their major prey species, such as the Orkney Vole, *Microtus arvalis orcadensis*, depend. Such changes are particularly detrimental to the males as it reduces the amount of food they can supply to the females early in the breeding season.

Box size: width 500 mm (19 ¾ in); height 200 mm (7 ¾ in)
Clutch size: 5
Collected: nest – 12 May 1894, Orkney mainland by ornithologist William Mark Pybus; eggs – 3 May 1893, Burry Brae, Ophir Orkney
Conservation status: Least Concern

Red-faced Mousebird

Urocolius indicus lacteifrons

Red-faced Mousebirds are highly sociable little birds found in the savannah, scrubland and open forests of central and southern Africa. Their habit of running, crouched like a mouse, along branches gives rise to the origin of their common name. Like many tropical birds, they can breed throughout the year but mainly at end of each dry season in the austral spring and summer. The nest is typically a large, untidy, open, deep-cup nest built on a foundation of dry thorn twigs and lined with grass, moss, some lichens and cobwebs. Mousebirds, on occasion, take advantage of the protection of nesting near wasp nests, for example *Belanogaster* sp., and also sometimes pull apart the nests of other birds, such as the loose, domed, dry grass stem nests built by the Cape Sparrow, to re-use as nesting materials.

Nest size: cup width 58 mm (2¼ in); cup depth 35 mm (1¼ in)
Clutch size: 3
Collected: 17 October 1905, Benguela, western Angola
by William John Ansorge (1850–1913)
Conservation status: Least Concern

Common Hoopoe

Upupa epops epops

The three hoopoe species are unmistakeable with both sexes having long, faded-orange crests tipped with black, which are often held erect, like an Edwardian fan. Their unusual name comes from their onomatopoeic dove-like call of 'hoo-poo-poo', each note identical in pitch and speed, and rapidly repeated. Common Hoopoe are widespread over Europe, Asia and Africa. They are notorious for choosing unusual nest sites and nest in any suitable hole in a wall, tree stump, cliff or rocks; they have even been found nesting in abandoned vehicles and a roll of abandoned carpet. Their nests can be both lined and unlined and are notoriously pungent due to the unusually strong uropygial gland secretions they spray on the nest as defence against predators. The European population of mature birds is estimated to be in the millions but hunting in southern Europe, together with potentially decreasing availability of nesting sites due to agricultural intensification, may lead to a decrease in the European population like that already witnessed in the northern Malay peninsula.

Nest size: width 208 mm (8 in); length 157 mm (6 in)
Clutch size: 6
Collected: 27 May 1883, Porto-Vecchio, southern Corsica by explorer John Whitehead (1860–1899)
Conservation status: Least Concern

Whitehead coll.
collector no.
14   6

MUS.
BRIT. J. A. Whitehead with Rothschild Bay.

Upupa epops epops.
Porto-Vecchio, Corsica.
27 May 1885.
John Whitehead.
Rothschild Bequest.

Buff-spotted Woodpecker

Campethera nivosa nivosa

You might think woodpeckers only make nest holes in trees, and most woodpecker species do, often excavating a new cavity each year, which in turn provide suitable nest holes for many other species. However, in areas with low numbers of trees or suitable sites to excavate, woodpeckers use other options like cacti or, in this case, an arboreal termite nest. Buff-spotted Woodpecker nests are often excavated in arboreal insect nests and this example from the early 1900s was considered especially remarkable. By the 1950s the same behaviour was also noted in species of kingfisher, parrots, trogons, puff-birds and a continga. In almost all instances the social insects involved were present when the nests were excavated. 'Dead' nests are seldom used as, without constant maintenance by the termites, the nests do not remain intact for long.

Nest size: termite nest diameter 149 mm (5 ¾ in)
Clutch size: 2
Collected: early 1900s, Efoulan, Cameroon by George Latimer Bates (1863–1940)
Conservation status: Least Concern

Red-fronted Tinkerbird

Pogoniulus pusillus affinis

The tiny Red-fronted Tinkerbird of east and southern Africa is part of the wider family of toucan-barbets, barbets and toucans. Like many of their relatives they nest in holes that they excavate out of dead wood. Red-fronted Tinkerbirds usually nest in fig, frangipani, *Acacia* or *Terminalia* trees. Here, the entire branch, including the excavated nest, has been collected from an old rubber tree. The narrow 2 cm (¾ in) entrance leads to a small chamber where the eggs were laid; the chamber is often excavated on the underside of a branch pointing upwards. This branch was so rotten that the collector was able to use a pocketknife to gently open it up and look at the nest. If you look carefully, you can still see the nail used to reseal the branch. Like many cavity nesting species, the eggs are white and unmarked.

Nest size: branch width 94 mm (3 ¾ in)
Clutch size: 2
Collected: nest – November 1909, near Dar es Salaam, Tanzania by Dr Leo von Boxberger (1879–1950);
eggs – July 1957, Ngeza, northern Tanzania
Conservation status: Least Concern

Black-headed Bee-eater

Merops breweri

Bee-eaters are some of the most spectacularly colourful and skilled aerial insectivores of the eastern hemisphere. They are expert hunters of flying insects and all nest in self-excavated tunnels, mostly in open savannah habitats, woodland edges and clearings, with the nests habitually littered with the vestiges of their insect prey. These two eggs and nest litter were extracted from the nest burrow of a Black-headed Bee-eater in Benue, Nigeria. The birds were only rediscovered in this region of southern Nigeria in January 1980, and this was the first time their nests had been scientifically described. Eight nest holes were found, each a 38–65 cm (15–26 in) long burrow, dug into the earth of a shallow ditch. At this nest site, the birds' prey were hawkmoths and cicadas, with some butterflies and beetles, and possibly grubs. However, more detailed study of the nest litter shown here revealed the remains of carpenter-bees, cetoniine beetles, such as the metallic flower beetle, *Plaesiorrhina recurva*, as well as worker Honeybees, *Apis mellifera*, and wasps (*Belanogaster* sp., *Chlorion maxillosum* and *Philanthus* sp.) and lastly ruteline beetles.

Glass vile size: width 25 mm (1 in)
Clutch size: 2
Collected: 29 March 1980, Itobe Road, Benue, Nigeria by J. A. Hendrick
Conservation status: Least Concern

Echo Parakeet

Psittacula eques echo

The Echo Parakeet of the montane forests of Mauritius is one of the greatest success stories of bird conservation. By 1986 the species was rapidly heading for extinction with a population thought to be less than 10 individuals. Almost all Old World parrots nest in some form of cavity and Echo Parakeets are no exception, nesting in holes in large trees like *Mimusops elengi*, often in a horizontal branch at least 10 m (33 ft) high. This small handful of seemingly inconsequential woodchips, and the remains of two eggs, were collected from a sheltered hole in a tree on the cloud shrouded Machabee Ridge in December 1987. At that time they were considered the rarest and most endangered bird of the Mascarene Islands. Dedicated monitoring and study of their last nest sites, at the beginning of a rigorous programme to manage the wild population linked to an extremely successful captive breeding programme, saved them. It would be difficult to find more poignant remnants than these to illustrate how the study of nests and combined efforts can save a species on the brink of extinction. Thankfully there are now hundreds of Echo Parakeets in the wild and their population continues to grow.

Box size: length 170 mm (6 ¾ in); width 115 mm (4 ½ in); height 40 mm (1 ½ in)
Clutch size: 2–4
Collected: December 1987, Machabee Ridge, Mauritius
Conservation status: Vulnerable

Superb Pitta

Pitta superba

The pittas are intensely colourful, secretive, rarely seen, birds of tropical and temperate forests in Asia and Africa. The glossy black of the Superb Pitta's body feathers contrast with its conspicuous blue and green wing feathers and bright red stomach feathers. It is only found on Manus Island, the largest of the Admiralty Islands in northern Papua New Guinea, and this unique nest specimen remains the only example known to science. Like most other pitta species, the male and female build a sizable spherical nest with a large side entrance measuring 11 x 7 cm (4 x 3 in). Rootlets, moss, leaves, twigs and decaying leaves are used to construct the main dome with the interior lined with nothing but rootlets and similar plant material. The two glossy white eggs are marked with small roundish purplish brown-black spots with underlying mauve-grey spots. During several research visits to Manus in the early 2000s, the Superb Pitta was not found where they had formerly been recorded or were only found at low numbers. When this nest was discovered in 1913 at least 29 birds were found in a two-month period. With much of Manus yet to be studied and explored, either the bird's major stronghold is yet to be found or they have suffered a steep decline in the intervening century. Logging, intense pressure from a growing human population, and threats from introduced cats and dogs, are all dangers to these mysterious little-known birds.

Nest size: width 260 mm (10 ¼ in); height 220 mm (8 ¾ in)
Clutch size: 2
Collected: 11 October 1913, Manus Island, Admiralty Islands, northern Papua New Guinea by Albert S. Meek (1871–1943)
Conservation status: Endangered

Dusky Broadbill

Corydon sumatranus

This remarkably distinctive but relatively small and compact example of the usually large, bag-like, pear-shaped nest of a Dusky Broadbill was found suspended from the end of a rattan palm 9 m (30 ft) from the ground and contained these three eggs with well-developed embryos. Dusky Broadbill are cooperative breeders with up to ten birds being recorded at a single nest. The nests are built by the adult pair and other members of the group and include a wide range of roots, epiphytes, leaves and moss. The outside can often be decorated with spider egg cases and insect cocoons and the entrance is usually about a third down from the top and almost hidden by a large 'porch'. The nests can be 2 m (6 ft) or more in length with an additional hanging tail of up to 70 cm (28 in). At only around 50 cm (20 in) long it is clear this example was trimmed dramatically for ease of transport after it was collected.

Nest size: width *c.* 300 mm (11¾ in); height *c.* 500 mm (19¾ in) (artificially shortened for ease of transport)
Clutch size: 2–4
Collected: 16 December 1904, near Sungai Tangli stream, western part of the Bentong District, border of Selangor state, Malaysia by Herbert C. Robinson (1874–1929)
Conservation status: Least Concern

Smithornis

Smithornis capensis
Petauke, Eastern Zambia.
9 March
1905.
Sheffield A. Neave (c)

N/115.1

African Broadbill

Smithornis capensis

The three broadbills found in Africa are closely related to the Green Broadbills of Asian forests. All live in tropical forests and relatively little is known of their breeding. This African Broadbill nest was found in dense bush on the banks of a stream in Petauke, eastern Zambia and the collector noted that the birds were known by the Nsenga people of Zambia and Mozambique as 'Tondowani'. It is a typical bag nest with a large side entrance, but without the commonly seen untidy hanging 'tail' that can be as long as 66 cm (26 in). In the wild, the nest is firmly attached to the twig it hangs from along its entire roof and the entrance faces away from the tree trunk. Broadbill nests can look very different depending on the nest materials available and choices made by the birds. Many 'brownish' nests, like this example, are woven from plants, dead leaves and twigs but black examples are woven from the long fibres of *Marismius* fungus, and some are even made entirely of beard lichens, *Usnea* sp., which gives them a rich pale green colour.

Nest size: width 106 mm (4 in); height 173 mm (6¾ in)
Clutch size: 1–3
Collected: 9 March 1905, dense bush on the banks of a stream in Petauke, eastern Zambia by Sheffield Airey Neave (1879–1961)
Conservation status: Least Concern

Golden-headed Manakin

Ceratopipra erythrocephala erythrocephala

The mankins are small fruit-eating birds of neotropical forests that typically build small cup nests, often from plant materials, suspended from a horizontal fork. This is a typical example of a Golden-headed Manakin nest and, like hummingbirds, the females undertake all the nest construction, incubation, care and feeding of the young. The nest is carefully constructed from rootlets and possibly the rhizomorphs of Marasmioid Basidiomycetes fungi, which is thin enough for the eggs to have been partially visible through the bottom of the nest. The fungi is also known as horse-hair fungi owing to the similarity of the fibres to long, black horse hairs. The fibres are thought by some to have antibiotic properties and can be longer and more flexible than other botanical materials. Consequently horse-hair fungi is widely used by hundreds of bird species in tropical forests, and research has shown it to have a significantly higher tensile strength and reduced water uptake than alternative fibres used to build nests.

Nest size: cup width 40 mm (1 ½ in); cup depth 15 mm (½ in)
Clutch size: 2
Collected: nest – 18 March 1970, Moco Moco, in the foothills of the Kanuku Mountain range, Rupununi Savannahs, Guyana by Dr Alan Lill; eggshells – 2 April 1970, same location
Conservation status: Least Concern

Pipra erythrocephala
LOC. *Moko-Moko, Kanuku M⁵;*
Guyana
DATE *18.2.70* ALT.
COLL. *Oystrow*

Green-and-black Fruiteater

Pipreola riefferii

The Green-and-black Fruiteater is a continga, a family which includes some of the most varied and colourful birds of tropical Central and South America. Sexual selection has resulted in a family of 65 species with significant variation in vocalization, plumage and behaviour. Their breeding biology is often poorly known and, what information is available, is largely concerned with the commoner species. One of the first significant ornithological collections from the northern Central Andes was made by the naturalist Thomas Knight Salmon (1841–1878). In 1878 he brought back an extraordinary series of 163 nests and eggs from Colombia including this nest built by the Green-and-black Fruiteater. Despite the birds' relative abundance, this substantial but lightweight cup nest remains one of the few fruiteater nests known to science. In the often torrential rain, humidity, and damp of a tropical rainforest it is important that nestlings are kept warm and relatively dry, so this nest, made entirely from moss and rootlets at a relatively high elevation, drains easily but is also substantial enough to conserve heat provided by the parent bird during incubation. When it was found the nest contained two eggs that were pale salmon-coloured with a few dark red spots.

Nest size: cup width 70 mm (2 ¾ in); cup depth 35 mm (1 ¼ in)
Clutch size: 2
Collected: 1870s near Santa Elena atop the Aburrá Valley, Antioquia, Colombia by Colonel Thomas K. Salmon (1840–1878)
Conservation status: Least Concern

43

MUS.
BRIT.

Pipreola rieffeni
antiquia
Colombia. *Cent*. *America*.
G. K. Salmon [P.]

Pipreola
rieffeni
Salmon
Antioquia.

REG. NO.   N. 197
PLATYRINCHU
9 MAY   1976
VENEZUEL

White-throated Spadebill

Platyrinchus mystaceus

The White-throated Spadebill is found across the Amazonian region. The species name *mystaceus* comes from the Latin for 'moustached' and is a reference to the broad, flat, wedge-shaped bill the bird uses to scoop prey from the undersides of leaves or twigs. The male sings when displaying with the yellow feathers on its head erected in a remarkable fan. The nest is a typical, smooth cone-like cup built in a forked branch and lined with black horse-hair fungal fibres, and the outer layer is constructed of pale-coloured dead leaves that drape below. This nest was found in seasonal deciduous forest at an elevation of about 400 m (1,300 ft) and was only 30 cm (12 in) above the ground in a sapling. It contained this single yellowish-white egg with very slight pale red spotting over the larger end.

Nest size: cup width 39 mm (1½ in); cup depth 27 mm (1 in)
Clutch size: 2
Collected: 9 May 1976, Rancho Grande National Park, Venezuela by Dr David William Snow (1924–2009)
Conservation status: Least Concern

Slaty-capped Flycatcher

Leptopogon superciliaris superciliaris

This is the globular nest built by a Slaty-capped Flycatcher. These small songbirds inhabit the humid montane forests and woodlands of South America from northern Venezuela south to Bolivia. This specimen was built by the subspecies living on the island of Trinidad and the northeastern coast of Venezuela. When describing its ecology, the collector George Smooker noted that it was built of a range of plant fibres well felted together, with always a certain number of parti-coloured cocoons on the outside, by which it can at once be recognized, and a lining of fine soft materials in the egg-chamber and an entrance hole at the side. The population is stable, but they remain rare to locally common but possibly locally extinct anywhere deforestation has been severe. Smooker noted: 'It is diminishing in numbers in proportion as the forest country is being opened up. To some extent it may escape observation owing to its habit of building in a dark place such as a deep cleft in a huge riverside boulder, or the little caves where earth has fallen away just under the top of a high bank at the side of a road and a fringe of vegetation hangs down the front like a screen.'

Nest size: width 93 mm (3 ½ in)
Clutch size: 2–3
Collected: 24 May 1926, foothill forests of the mountain of Morne Bleu, Trinidad by G. D. Smooker
Conservation status: Least Concern

Texas Bound. Surv. J. H. Clark, Comm'r.
3908   56
Milvulus
Forficatus.
May 25 .60
H Cobb
                        Chas. S. McCarthy,

Scissor-tailed Flycatcher

Tyrannus forficatus

Tyrant-Flycatchers have one of the most diverse nesting architectures in the Americas. Many species build open-cup nests, whilst others build globular, or domed nests and some nest in cavities. This is a typical open-cup nest of the Scissor-tailed Flycatcher. These relatively short-distance migrants have a long-breeding season. The female that built this nest in 1860 would have left her wintering grounds in southern Mexico and Central America in March and arrived in Oklahoma, USA in early April. Accordingly, the earliest observations of nest building in Oklahoma are usually from mid-April. The analysis of 241 historical museum egg sets like these allowed researchers to determine that the mean date the first egg is laid (the clutch initiation date) is 22 May. Their close-knit cup nests commonly include cudweed, and the female can also use post oak catkins (male flowers produced in the spring), both of which seem to be present here. A variety of materials can be used to line their nests, for example the feathery pappus down of the Virginia Thistle, but the most common lining is dried rootlets. Anthropogenic materials like pieces of string, thread and cloth were noticed in their nests as early as the 1950s.

Nest size: cup width 60 mm (2 ¼ in); cup depth 40 mm (1 ½ in)
Clutch size: 3
Collected: 25 May 1860, Fort Cobb, Caddo, Oklahoma, USA
by Charles S. McCarthy and John Henry Clark
Conservation status: Least Concern

San Cristóbal Vermilion Flycatcher

Pyrocephalus rubinus dubius

In 2016 the San Cristóbal Vermilion Flycatcher, a subspecies of the Vermilion Flycatcher, was described as the first avian extinction of the Galápagos Islands. This was a widespread species and all build a shallow cup of twigs and grasses, lined with down, feathers and hair. The male strongly influences where the nest is built by displaying at its preferred location, but the nest is generally built by the female. San Cristóbal is the easternmost island of the Galápagos archipelago and the fifth largest. During the South Sea zoological expedition of Gifford Pinchot (an American forester and politician) in 1929, the birds were recorded as plentiful, but by the 1980s they were rare. It was thought that the last confirmed records of the species on the island dated to the 1980s, but research in 2019 showed that local people may have encountered the birds between 1976 and 2016. It is now considered that, at best, a handful may have survived until recently, but it is likely that their final extinction occurred within the last decade.

Nest size: cup width 40 mm (1½ in); cup depth 18 mm (0.07 in)
Clutch size: 2–3
Collected: 15 March 1901, San Cristóbal in Ecuador's Galápagos Islands
Conservation status: Extinct

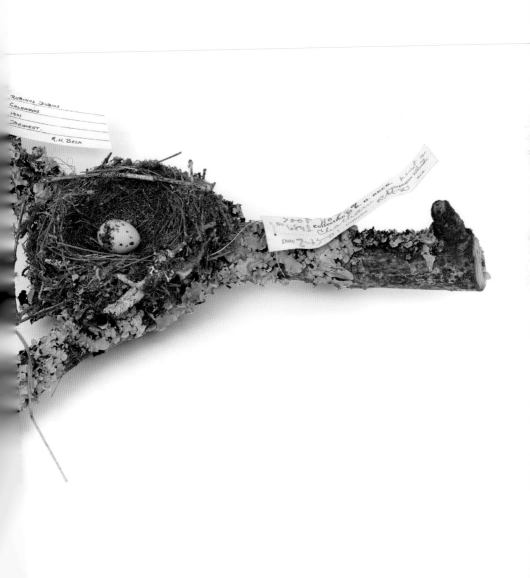

Great Antshrike

Taraba major semifasciatus

The Great Antshrike is a member of a large family of neotropical birds of dense forests known as antbirds. Some eat ants, but not all, so the name is a little misleading. Some are cooperative breeders with young birds, usually males from previous nests, staying to help the breeding adults raise another brood. Their nests are generally open cups, made of twigs, stems, leaves and rootlets, often suspended by the rim in the fork of a tree branch. The Great Antshrike is a bird of dense forest thicket, savannah woodland and clearings in evergreen forests from eastern Mexico to northern Argentina, and the nests of the different subspecies differ slightly in their construction. Trinidadian examples are deep, pensile cups, suspended below horizontal forks or crossed vines, often interwoven with black horse-hair fungal fibres and lightly constructed and gracile.

Nest size: cup width *c.* 70 mm (2¾ in); cup depth *c.* 65 mm (2½ in)
Clutch size: 2–3
Collected: nest – 12 April 1970, island of Trinidad by Dr David W. Snow (1924–2009); eggs – 18 June 1933, Orinola, Trinidad
Conservation: Least Concern

BRIT. MUS.
Taraba major
Trinidad 12.4.70 . S.4

Taroba major
Trinidad
12 April 1970.

D. Snow.

Rufous Hornero

Furnarius rufus

Rufous Hornero are in the family of ovenbirds and woodcreepers, and all build enclosed nests. But the way each species achieves this shows a greater diversity of nest building than any other bird family. The large, distinctive, spherical 'adobe oven' nests built by the Rufous Hornero of South America are perhaps the ultimate expression of a covered nest (the Spanish word horno means 'oven'). They are arguably some of the most recognizable and iconic structures in all avian architecture. The 3–5 cm (1–2 in) thick walls are built from clay and mud, often with some dung and dry grasses – the equivalent of a human building a 2.5 m (8 ft) high, domed mud structure with 50 cm (20 in) thick walls, weighing as much as an elephant. This 19th century example may have taken up to 12 weeks to build but hornero nests can be constructed in as little as 15 days. The entrance is usually orientated away from the prevailing wind, and the nest chamber is lined with grasses and stems into which four white eggs are laid. Rufous Hornero nests can be eclectically placed on almost any structure including tree branches, fence posts, or even on or in the sun-bleached skull of a large mammal.

Nest size: width 252 mm (10 in); height 201 mm (8 in)
Clutch size: 4
Collected: late 1800s, South America
Conservation: Least Concern

Prince Albert's Lyrebird

Menura alberti

Albert's Lyrebird, the rarer of the two known lyrebird species, is restricted to wet forests in Queensland and New South Wales, Australia. Little is known of their breeding and this nest, described by ornithologist John Gould in 1853, was the first known to European science. In the intervening 170 years it has collapsed, but Gould noted: 'The nest was oven-shaped in form; outwardly constructed of roots, tendrils and leaves of palms, and lined with green mosses. It was about 2 feet in length by 16 inches in breadth, domed over except at one end. The eggs, barely 2¼ inches long by 1¾ broad, are of a deep purplish chocolate, irregularly blotched and freckled with a darker colour.' In a letter to Gould, the collector wrote: 'It gives me much pleasure to forward to you the nest and egg of Menura alberti, [...] It was placed on a rocky ledge, about one hundred feet above the stream, [...] Another nest was also found in the brush near the water; it would seem, therefore, that there is no rule as to the elevation of the locality in which it is placed. Only one egg was found in each nest; and, from all the information I could glean on the subject, the bird never lays but one.' He was right and Albert's Lyrebird only lay one egg. The illustration, taken from the *Proceedings of the Zoological Society of London* (1853), clearly shows how Gould interpreted the nest he was sent, but mistakenly shows the two eggs placed in the same nest.

Nest size: width *c.* 375 mm (14 ¾ in)
Clutch size: 1
Collected: possibly 26 September 1852, Richmond River, New South Wales, Australia by James Fowler Wilcox (1823–1881)
Conservation: Least Concern

Tooth-billed Bowerbird

Scenopoeetes dentirostris

The bowerbirds are more famous for the extraordinary and distinctive structures they build to attract a mate than for their nests. However, the Tooth-billed Bowerbird, also known as the Stagemaker or Cherra-chelbo by the Yidinji people of far north Queensland, Australia doesn't build a bower structure. Rather they seasonally clear and decorate a 2 m (6½ ft) long oval 'court' where the male arranges leaves, such as from Ivory Basswood, silverside up on the ground. Often the courts are situated near to display trees, which the male hides behind to give a vocal display before rushing at the female with a series of animated postures. Their nests are, in comparison, somewhat muted, sparse platforms of twigs lined with finer shoots. This important example, collected during an expedition to north Queensland led by Sidney Jackson and Ted Frizelle in 1909, was amongst the first discovered of this enigmatic species. It is still held together by the string they sewed through it for transport. Collecting it was difficult and dangerous so the expertise and assistance of several Yidinji collectors was critical to their eventual success. Jackson acknowledged that: 'their [the Yidinji] climbing skills and their local knowledge of places, birds, and animals was exceedingly useful.'

Nest size: width 166 mm (6 ½ in)
Clutch size: 2
Collected: 1909, northeastern Queensland, Australia, Yidinji naturalists working with Sidney Jackson and Ted Frizelle
Conservation: Near Threatened

Southern Emu-Wren

Stipiturus malachurus westernensis

The Southern Emu-Wren is one of the family of fairywrens of Australia and New Guinea. The term 'fairywren' is seemingly a 20th century name, used to distinguish these delicate, lively wren-like birds from their distant cousins, the wrens (Troglodytidae, see p.236). All the fairywren species live in groups, often with cooperative breeding, and the majority build domed nests and that includes the Southern Emu-Wren shown here. The nest would have originally been an unambiguously domed oval with a side entrance but, like many older museum nests, the original shape has been distorted over time. This example was given to the collections in 1842 by ornithologist John Gould who described it: '... a small ball-shaped structure, with rather a large opening on one side, is composed of grasses lined with feathers, and artfully concealed in a tuft of grass or low shrub. One that I found in Recherche Bay contained three newly hatched young: this being the only nest I ever met with, I am unable to give any description of its eggs, but I am informed they are always three in number.'

Nest size: width 84 mm (3 ¼ in)
Clutch size: 2–4
Collected: probably May 1841
Conservation: Least Concern

MYZOMELA SCLATERI
VUATOM, NEW BRITAIN
FEB 1928   OTTO MEYER [C]

B.M.
(N.H.)

Sclater's Myzomela

Myzomela sclateri

Sclater's Myzomela is a member of a large, diverse Australo-Papuan family known as honeyeaters. All known nests are cup-shaped structures of varying complexity; this is a simple example built by the little-known honeyeater Sclater's Myzomela. It is a coarsely woven, thin-walled cup into which two, spotted, pale salmon pink eggs have been laid. The generic name *Myzomela* is derived from the Greek words myzo 'to suckle' and meli 'honey'. The markedly decurved bills seen in several honeyeaters and sunbirds probably evolved to enable the birds to reach flowers at the ends of branches more easily. Consistent differences in bill length between the sexes of some nectarivorous species suggest that males and females may exploit different flowers. The tongues of honeyeaters are broad and brush-tipped to allow the collection of nectar. Brush-tipped tongues can cover large areas on each lick, and this may also allow them to exploit the thinly spread nectar and honeydew within large flowers. However, all nectar-feeding birds also need additional food sources such as insects and other invertebrates as nectar, whilst full of energy, is a very poor source of protein.

Nest size: cup width 32 mm (1¼ in); cup depth 38 mm (1½ in)
Clutch size: 2
Collected: February 1928, Watom Island off northern coast of New Britian, Papua New Guinea by Father Otto Meyer (1877–1937)
Conservation: Least Concern

Yellow-rumped Thornbill

Acanthiza chrysorrhoa leighi

The thornbills are small, rather dull-coloured, insectivorous songbirds of Australia and New Guinea. Some, like the Gerygone species, build hanging, often tailed, nests but others build bulky and untidy domed structures with side entrances, like these remains of the domed nest built by a Yellow-rumped Thornbill. It is typically constructed from dried grass, bark fibres, leaves and rootlets, bound together with spiders' webs and laboriously lined with grass and feathers, though the nests usually have a side entrance and are more cup-shaped. It is built by both sexes and nests can take up to four weeks to build. 'False nests' can be built on top or at the side of the main chamber. The purpose of these false nests is unclear but different theories have been suggested. Some ornithologists believe that building 'false' nests is simply practise, i.e. repeatedly building to acquire or improve technique. Others have suggested they are an attempt at misleading predators or brood-parasites, roosting sites for the male or fledglings, or simply a consequence of the male's obsessive desire to build in the breeding season. More research may confirm one of these ideas or give an entirely new, yet unknown, reason for the behaviour.

Nest size: cup width and depth 50 mm (2 in)
Clutch size: 3–4
Collected: late 1800s, Victoria, Australia
Conservation: Least Concern

Order *Passeres*
Genus *Geobasileus*
Species *chrysorrhœa*
Common Name *Yellow rumped Geobasileus*
Locality *Victoria*

MUS
BRIT

Geobasileus. chrysorrhœa.
Victoria . N. S. Wales
The Government of Victoria [P.]

Grey-crowned Babbler

Pomatostomus temporalis temporalis

The Grey-crowned Babbler, like other Australasian babblers, resemble the scimitar babblers of Asia though they are distantly related. Their bodies have evolved to look superficially alike as they have similar feeding habits, for example gleaning or probing bark and foraging on the ground using their bills to turn leaves and stones for prey. All five species of pseudo-babbler build multiple, large, domed nests which, unusually, are used to incubate eggs, raise young and for roosting throughout the year by the whole family group. Their nests can be very large, such as the flask-shaped pendent nest of the Papuan Babbler, *Garritornis isidorei,* of New Guinea, which can be up to 2 m (6½ ft) in length. It is difficult to envisage now exactly how this Grey-crowned Babbler nest looked in situ and that illustrates a perennial problem for ornithologists studying historical nests. Time, and the inevitable distortion caused by packing and travel can make it difficult to discern a nest's original shape. This would have been a large dome of sticks when built, constructed cooperatively by the monogamous breeding pair with 'helpers' – usually siblings or previous offspring.

Nest size: total width *c.* 457 mm (18 in)
Clutch size: 2–6
Collected: nest – late 1800s; eggs – 16 October 1884; Victoria, Australia
Conservation: Least Concern

Spectacled Longbill

Oedistoma iliolophus fergussonis

The eleven species of berrypeckers and longbills from New Guinea make up one of the most poorly known families in ornithology. Perhaps unsurprisingly this Spectacled Longbill nest is an absolute rarity and remains the only known research specimen. When *Melilestes fergussonis* (now *Oedistoma iliolophus fergussonis*) was scientifically described in 1896 from bird specimens collected alongside this nest, the bird curator at the Natural History Museum Tring, Ernst Hartert also gave a detailed description of this specific nest: 'A nest was found in December. It is fastened to some leaves and a thin twig. I should say spun on to it, and outside covered with half-decayed dry leaves. It is rather small for the bird, and consists chiefly of dry grass, but is inside thickly lined with very soft snow-white vegetable silk. It had one egg, which is creamy white, with some pale reddish spots all over, and with a close ring of pale brownish red spots and dots near the broader end, as well as a few deep brown hairlines encircling the egg above the middle. It measures 20 x 14.3 mm.' The breeding of this family is virtually unknown, despite some species being widespread, their cryptic colouring perhaps contributing to them often being overlooked.

Nest size: cup width 40 mm (1½ in); cup depth 30 mm (1 in)
Clutch size: 1-2
Collected: 5 December 1894, New Guinea
by Albert S. Meek (1871–1943)
Conservation: Least Concern

Melilestes fuscossonia

South Island Saddleback/Tīeke

Philesturnus carunculatus

The kokakos, saddlebacks and extinct Huia all have wattles at the base of the bill, and all were once common across New Zealand. Three species are now only found in predator-free areas, the South Island Kokako is almost certainly lost, and the Huia was extinct by the early 1900s. This South Island Saddleback nest was built by the female in a natural cavity. Twigs and leaves were brought together and loosely bound and lined with inner bark fibres, grasses and tree-fern scales. Stephens Island/Takapourewa, where this nest was probably found, is a tiny but mountainous island at the northern tip of the Marlborough Sounds in the South Island. Today the island's forest has been described as a 'ghost town' but 130 years ago, when this nest was collected, it was alive with at least 12 bird species that are no longer found there. The island is sadly most infamous for the loss of the world's only flightless passerine, the tiny endemic Stephens Island Wren, in 1895. Its extinction was notoriously linked to a single cat belonging to the lighthouse keeper at the time. However, a single cat was not the only culprit, and the situation was clearly exacerbated by a wild population of cats established during the building of the lighthouse, which started operating in January 1894. Today, in an ongoing conservation process started in 1964, saddlebacks are still being translocated from islands with stable populations to other predator-free locations like Mokiiti (Little Moggy) Island and Rerewhakaupoko (Solomon) Island.

Nest size: cup width 80 mm (3 in); cup depth 10 mm (½ in)
Clutch size: 3
Collected: probably January 1893, Takapourewa
(Stephens Island), Cook Strait, New Zealand
Conservation: Least Concern

Andaman Large Cuckooshrike

Coracina javensis andamana

This nest of the Andaman Large Cuckooshrike is a typical, small, 9 cm (3½ in) diameter shallow cup nest constructed from twigs and bark fragments held together with cobwebs. The Andamanese avifauna are all descended from species that have crossed permanent water barriers to colonize the archipelago. The Andaman and Nicobar Islands support 13 endemic species and around 86 endemic subspecies. Relatively little is known of this cuckooshrike's ecology, and this is a major priority for future research, both on the species and many members of the family.

Nest size: cup width 70 mm (2¾ in); cup depth 10 mm (½ in)
Clutch size: 2–3
Collected: nest – 4 June 1905, near Port Blair, Andaman Islands by Bertram B. Osmaston (1868-1961); eggs – February 1907, same location
Conservation: Least Concern

Spotted Quail-thrush

Cinclosoma punctatum dovei

This bird comes from a small family, the jewel-babblers and quail-thrushes, whose breeding ecology is generally poorly known. Jewel-babblers are medium-sized songbirds of the wet forests of New Guinea and neighbouring islands, whereas the quail-thrushes generally prefer dry woods and scrubland in Australia and New Guinea. Of what we know so far, most seem to build simple, open-cup nests. This small box and its contents are all that remain of the first Spotted Quail-thrush nest gathered for science. The female built a loosely constructed pad of dry grass, leaves and bark strips, described by ornithologist John Gould in 1848: 'The nest is a slight and rather careless structure, composed of leaves and the inner bark of trees, and is of a round open form; it is always placed on the ground, under the shelter of a large stone, stump of a tree, or a tuft of grass'. Today, this modest pad of twigs and leaves is the Museum's earliest known example of the remains of a bird's nest from Australia and an important milestone in the history of ornithology.

Box size: width 110 mm (4¼ in); height 60 mm (2¼ in)
Clutch size: 2–3
Collected: nest – 14 November 1838, South Arm Peninsula, near Hobart, Tasmania; eggs – possibly collected at the same time
Conservation: Least Concern

Rusty Pitohui

Pseudorectes ferrugineus ferrugineus

The Rusty, White-bellied and Black Pitohui, Whistlers and their relatives are mostly found in Australasia with a few species in the Indomalayan region. Their nests are characteristically bulky, lined cups. This example, built by the Rusty Pitohui of Western Papua, constructed of woody vines, sticks, dead leaves and rootlets, is typical. The name 'pitohui' is used for several morphologically similar but quite distantly related birds, which we now know form an ecological, rather than evolutionary related group. The name is onomatopoeic and is also a Papuan term which means 'rubbish' – like the Blue-capped Ifrita (see p.150), several pitohuis produce a powerful neurotoxin in their feathers that makes them inedible, so the name is likely to be a reference to their unpleasant taste. This specimen was collected with the help of the Kamoro people. A naturalist on the expedition, during which this nest was collected, noted that rainfall is so heavy and constant in the neighbourhood of the mountains here that the year is essentially one long wet season. Breeding is often timed to coincide with the wet season so this means the birds may have multiple opportunities to breed each year.

Nest size: cup width 90 mm (3½ in); cup depth 50 mm (2 in)
Clutch size: 1
Collected: 19 December 1912, near Parimau, on the Mimika River, western New Guinea by Claude Henry Baxter Grant (1878–1958)
Conservation: Least Concern

Rufous-naped Bellbird

Aleadryas rufinucha niveifrons

The three Australo-Papuan bellbirds are named for their rhythmically repeating multi-part songs. Like their close relatives the whistlers and allies, they build open-cup nests in the fork of trees, primarily of moss, bark, leaves and rootlets. This is a rare example of a nest and egg of a Rufous-naped Bellbird. The closely related Crested Bellbird, *Oreoica gutturalis*, of Australia builds a similar deep-cup nest and, unusually, they habitually add poisonous hairy caterpillars, such as the anthelid *Anthela ocellata*, to the nest. These are often alive but paralyzed and frequently added along the rim or built into the bottom of the nest before or during egg-laying. Many Australian caterpillars produce pain-inducing venoms and some have evolved biological defences such as irritative hairs and toxins that make them poisonous to eat. The exact reason for adding these caterpillars to the nests is unclear but the Australian naturalist Alexander Chisolm was one of the first to report this behaviour in 1918 and he intriguingly noted that, when threatened, the chicks stretch out their necks and wave their heads in the same threatening manner as the tails of processional caterpillars. He concluded the adults and chicks may have evolved both behaviours as defence but a century later it remains unclear as to whether the caterpillars are a food source or an unusual nest protection. Whether the Rufous-naped Bellbird sometimes uses poisonous caterpillars like their Australian relatives is yet to be determined.

Nest size: cup width 60 mm (2¼ in); cup depth 55 mm (2¼ in)
Clutch size: 1–2
Collected: 27 December 1940, Boneno, Mt. Mura, 30 miles northwest of Mt. Simpson, Central Dividing, Milne Bay, Papua New Guinea by Frederick W. Shaw Mayer (1899–1989)
Conservation: Least Concern

Rufous-browed Peppershrike

Cyclarhis gujanensis flavipectus

The Rufous-browed Peppershrike is one of the larger species in the vireo family, with a huge distribution from the forests of Mexico south to similar habitats in Uruguay. It is a family of small, sometimes highly vocal, occasionally distinctively coloured, forest birds and most build cup nests that are supported between horizontal forked branches. The collector, George K. Cherrie, described another nest he found of the same species in the Orinoco region: 'In 1907 I found a nest at La Cascabel (near the mouth of the San Feliz on the Cuchivero River) on the 23rd day of May. The nest was situated in a Chaparro oak that stood near the edge of an extensive open savannah. It was placed at the extreme tip of a long horizontal limb, about 4.5 m (15 ft) from the ground, suspended between forked twigs. For a pendant nest it was unusually shallow; the walls thin, and it might be described almost as a net woven between the forks and sagging in the centre. Outwardly it was composed entirely of soft grasses, and there was an inner lining of a very few hair-like vegetable fibres. The attachment to the supporting twigs was slight and frail looking. The nest walls were so thin and the meshes so open, that the eggs were visible when looking from the ground through the bottom of the nest.'

Nest size: cup width 65 mm (2 ½ in); cup depth 35 mm (1 ¼ in)
Clutch size: 1
Collected: 28 August 1898, near La Urbana, Orinoco River in Bolívar, eastern Venezuela
Conservation: Least Concern

Stephens Island/Takapourewa Piopio

Turnagra capensis minor

The two extinct piopio species were endemic to New Zealand. Their evolutionary relationship to the rest of the songbirds has been hotly debated for over a century, but recent DNA research has shown that they are, in fact, genetically related to the orioles (the Old World orioles are songbirds found in wooded habitats across parts of Europe, Africa, Asia and Australasia). Whilst piopio and the other Australasian orioles have a far duller, olive-brown plumage than their vibrant black-and-yellow cousins, their eggs and nests are similar. This extremely rare and irreplaceable extinct South Island Piopio nest is one of only six known in collections worldwide. It is, as far as we can tell, a representative example of their cup-shaped nest of small dry twigs with bark, lined with grass. The exact history of this nest is unclear but, as the handwriting on the label matches that of the South Island Saddleback nest (see p.110), this could suggest it may have been collected during an austral summer in the early 1890s on Stephens Island/Takapourewa, South Island. The island hosted a unique endemic subspecies of piopio, *Turnagra capensis minor*, which flourished until the mid-1890s and then suffered the same fate as the endemic Stephens Island Wren and the island's South Island Saddleback population. Another sad casualty of the cats introduced to the island by the building of the lighthouse in the 1890s.

Nest size: cup width 70 mm (2 ¾ in); cup depth 30 mm (1 in)
Clutch size: 2
Collected: possibly in an austral summer in the early 1890s, Takapourewa (Stephen's Island), at the northernmost tip of the Marlborough Sounds, South Island, New Zealand
Conservation: Extinct

Black-breasted Boatbill

Machaerirhynchus nigripectus harterti

The two boatbill species are small, black and yellow birds of the rainforests of northern Australia and New Guinea, and the behaviour and breeding biology of both are poorly studied. Their unusually flattened bills have a distinct 'keel' on the upper mandible resembling an upturned rowing boat. Both species are primarily insectivorous, and it may be that their bills act like a 'catcher's mitt' – a larger, flattened bill that increases the total capture area for smaller prey, a suggestion proposed by the American evolutionary biologist and ornithologist Douglas W. Mock (1933–2022) in 1975 to explain the similarly-shaped bill belonging to the Boat-billed Heron, *Cochlearius cochlearius*. The Black-breasted Boatbill, endemic to the montane and submontane forest of New Guinea, is the least well-known of the two species. This nest is built using the fibres from the base of tree fern fronds, bound together with spiders' webs, with the exterior decorated with lichen, and has a small, deep cup in the centre. It was placed in a fork in a branch about 3 m (10 ft) from the ground.

Nest size: cup 30 x 30 mm (1 x 1 in)
Clutch size: 2
Collected: 20 December 1940, Mount Mura, Boneno on the southeastern peninsula of New Guinea by Frederick W. Shaw Mayer (1899–1989)
Conservation: Least Concern

Gray Butcherbird

Cracticus torquatus cinereus

The woodswallows, butcherbirds, Australian magpie and allies are intermediate to large songbirds of Australia and Southeast Asia. All build relatively simple cup nests of twigs lined with finer materials like grasses. This typical nest of the Tasmanian Gray Butcherbird was almost certainly the first collected for science. Its survival, after 200 years, is a marvel as many nests donated during the 1800s have long-since perished. Writing in 1909 the Tasmanian ornithologist Ernest Harrison gave a detailed account of their nests: 'The nest of the Tasmanian Butcherbird is built of thin dry twigs put together compactly but lightly. Considering the material, it is very neatly made and is not thick or bulky; looked at from below the light can be seen all through it. The interior is a deep, very symmetrical saucer-shaped depression neatly lined with root fibre, etc. I have usually found the nest in rather stunted young gum trees, built in a clump of small branches on the side of the stem, and about fifteen or twenty feet from the ground. A small dry gully on a steep hillside is a favourite place.'

Nest size: cup width 95 mm (3¾ in); cup depth 40 mm (1½ in)
Clutch size: 3–4
Collected: 8 October 1838, Tasmania
Conservation: Least Concern

Boulton's Batis

Batis margaritae margaritae

The 31 species of boldly-patterned wattle-eyes and batises are all found in the forests and woodlands of sub-Saharan Africa. Their nests are all similar structures and built by both the male and the female. Boulton's (or Margaret's) Batis was first discovered in February 1931 by Rudyerd and Laura Boulton during the Pulitzer Angola Expedition for the Carnegie Museum of Natural History, USA. These little black, grey and white songbirds have a small range in Angola and Zambia, with this subspecies inhabiting the evergreen Mavunda forests of the upper slopes of Mount Moco, the highest mountain in Angola. Until this nest was located their nest and eggs had never been described and this remains the only nest available for study. This small, cup-shaped nest was found in the fork of a sapling *c.* 90 cm (35 in) from the ground within an area of dense undergrowth. It contained two creamy white eggs covered with dark and pale brown irregular blotches. The nest is constructed from grass and moss and lined with fine grass, and the exterior deftly camouflaged using small pieces of lichens held in place with spiders' webs. Like all batises and wattle-eyes the birds' diet comprises a diverse array of insect prey gleaned from trees and vegetation.

Nest size: overall width 80 mm (3 in); height 90 mm (3½ in)
Clutch size: 2
Collected: 7 August 2010, Mount Moco, Angola
by Michael Mills and Alexandre Vaz
Conservation: Least Concern

Banded Wattle-eye

Platysteira laticincta

The endangered Banded Wattle-eye is only found in the Bamenda Highlands of western Cameroon. It breeds in the early dry season and this small cup nest of mosses and other plant materials is encased in spiders' webs and bark strips. Found during a research trip to study the birds of the Kilum-Ijim forest, this is arguably the species' last stronghold, and the largest remaining area of Afromontane forest in West Africa. Between 1965 and 1985 extensive deforestation destroyed at least 50 per cent of the birds' remaining habitat on Mount Oku and by 1985 it was feared their extinction was almost inevitable. Thankfully a joint project between BirdLife International and the Cameroon Government has helped protect the remaining montane forest, and community-based conservation has been extended to other forest fragments in the Bamenda Highlands. Even so, they remain threatened by fires, forest clearance and increased predation of nests at the edge of the remaining forest fragments.

Nest size: cup width 40 mm (1½ in); cup depth 18 mm (0.7 in)
Clutch size: 1–3
Collected: 2 January 1989, Mount Oku, near Jikijem, north side of Lake Oku, Bui, northwest Cameroon, Africa by John Parrott
Conservation: Endangered

Madagascar Blue Vanga

*Cyanolanius madagascarinus
madagascarinus*

Exactly which species belong in the Vangidae family has been debated by ornithologists. Historically the family included only species endemic to Madagascar, but recent research on their evolutionary relationships have included the helmetshrikes of Africa and a group of African and Southeast Asian species such as woodshrikes, shrike-flycatchers and flycatcher-shrikes. This nest was built by one of the most stunning birds in Madagascar, the Madagascar Blue Vanga. Their nesting wasn't formally described in detail until 1970 so this 1920s example is almost certainly the first nest of the species collected for science. It is a compact, closely woven 3.5 cm (1½ in) deep cup built tightly within a tree fork. Thin twigs, grasses and other plant material have been held together with copious quantities of spiders' webs and lined with fine grasses. The outside is decorated extensively with lichens held on with more arthropod silk. One pale bluish egg with small lilac-grey to red-brown speckles was found in the nest. At the time it was built this would have been a vibrant green structure that has become somewhat muted over time.

Nest size: cup width 45 mm (1¾ in); cup depth 35 mm (1½ in)
Clutch size: largely unknown but may be 2–5 normally
Collected: December 1923, near Rogez, Vohibinany district of eastern Madagascar
Conservation: Least Concern

no 1. *Artamia bicolor*
Roseg. 1. madagascar. Dec 1913
with 1 egg

Ægithina tiphia

Siam

(Sir Walter Williamson)

Rothschild Bequest

1914 - 23

Common Iora

Aegithina tiphia horizoptera

The Common Iora is one of four species of boldly-coloured, insectivorous birds found in the woodlands and shrubland habitats of Asia. All the ioras build small, neat, relatively deep, cup nests of grass and rootlets held together with arthropod silk. The cup is thick-walled and steep-sided, made of botanical fibres such as tendrils and grasses all carefully felted together with spiders' webs. Their nests have been described as some of the most exquisite in Southeast Asia. The species' unusually melancholic, often unmusical, calls are often commented on. Whilst they produce a great variety of notes, the most prominent is a prolonged 'we-e-e-e-tu' a long, drawn-out wail with the last note dropping suddenly. Apparently, this call is rare and largely occurs in the rains, and the eminent British ornithologist, E.C. Stuart-Baker noted that 'when constantly repeated to the accompaniment of the splash and the sough of the wind, is one of the saddest little bird-notes imaginable.' The two eggs shown were laid in this nest, but Common Ioras are often parasitized by the Banded Bay Cuckoo, *Cacomantis sonneratii*, over much of their range.

Nest size: cup width 40 mm (1½ in); cup depth 30 mm (1 in)
Clutch size: 2
Collected: 15 April 1920, Bangkok, Thailand
by Sir Walter J. Williamson (1867–1954)
Conservation: Least Concern

Bokmakierie

Telophorus zeylonus zeylonus

We still have a great deal to learn regarding the breeding of the bush-shrikes, puffbacks and tchagras of sub-Saharan Africa. All members of the family seem to build flimsy cup or saucer-shaped twig nests. This example, built by a bush-shrike called the Bokmakierie, would have been built by both sexes. It is a compact and neat bowl, carefully lined with fine rootlets and the fluffy *Eriocephalus* seed material used by many South African birds. There is thought to be a mutualism between birds and *Eriocephalus* plants in southern Africa. For example, the breeding of Karoo Prinia, *Prinia maculosa*, and the seed fluff production are associated – the seed fluff availability precisely coinciding with nest building in prinias. This may suggest an evolutionary relationship that benefits both, as *Eriocephalus* seed material is available for dispersal just as the birds are breeding. But the interaction between birds and *Eriocephalus* is not simple because the benefit for the plants largely depends on the species of birds gathering the seed material. Nevertheless, it is an interesting and possibly phenologically linked interaction, which, if disrupted by anthropogenic climate change, might affect nest building and breeding success for species that rely on this naturally fluffy seed material.

Nest size: cup width 80 mm (3 in); cup depth 40 mm (1½ in)
Clutch size: 2–6 usually 3
Collected: 13 December 1903, near Johannesburg, South Africa
Conservation: Least Concern

Aldabra Drongo

Dicrurus aldabranus

The beautiful, black, blue and grey drongos are glossy feathered, flycatching birds of Africa, Asia and Australia. All build cup nests of grasses, rootlets and tendrils, often, as in this case, suspended from a horizontal fork. This typical example was built by the Aldabra Drongo, endemic to the Aldabra Atoll in the southwestern Seychelles. It is a skilfully rounded, shallow cup made from intertwined plant fibres, especially casuarina needles and grass leaves, bound together with cobweb. Aldabra's remote location in the Indian Ocean, lack of freshwater and dense scrub afforded it relative protection from human interferance, but exploitation of the turtles, tortoises and birds began as soon as the first settlement was established in the 1880s. In the 1960s a new threat emerged with plans to create an air force base on the islands. The campaign to save Aldabra's delicate ecosystem, led by the Royal Society, was one of the first internationally successful conservation campaigns. The research on the islands' flora and fauna that followed, of which this specimen is part, ultimately led to the protection of the islands in 1981 and they became a UNESCO world heritage site in 1982.

Nest size: cup width 80 mm (3 in); cup depth 30 mm (1 in)
Clutch size: 1–3
Collected: 23 November 1967, western extremity of Malabar (Middle Island), Johnny Channel or Gionnet, Aldabra Atoll, southwestern Seychelles
Conservation: Near Threatened

Long-tailed Fantail

Rhipidura opistherythra

The fantails of Australasian and South Asian forests are named for their habit of rapidly fanning their tail feathers to flush out insects for food. The nests of fantails are all relatively similar – a small, neat cup built of grass and stems, held together with spiders' webs. This nest, built by the Long-tailed Fantail of the Tanimbar Islands, Indonesia, was collected over a century ago but never formally described. Many fantail nests are deep cups, but this is a shallower, old-style champagne saucer shape, wider than it is deep and measuring 68 mm. (2 ½ in) at its widest with a cup that is only 19 mm (½ in) deep. Like most fantail nests it also has a short but distinct 'tail' measuring 50 mm (2 in). When it was found it held these two cream eggs, each with a band of rusty brown and pale ash-grey spots near the blunt end. The collector of the nest, Heinrich Kühn, noted in 1901 that 'much of the Islands are very thickly populated, and accordingly very much of the soil is under culture.' Recent descriptions have shown logging has been reported in southern parts of Yamdena, the largest island in the group, and the loss of primary forest habitat may yet threaten their future.

Nest size: nest cup width 45 mm (1 ¾ mm);
nest cup depth 19 mm (½ in)
Clutch size: 2
Collected: 13 January 1901, far western coast of Larat Island, Tanimbar Islands, Maluku province, Indonesia by Heinrich Kühn
Conservation: Near Threatened

Masked Shrike

Lanius nubicus

The shrikes are songbirds that have evolved as highly efficient daytime hunters in a variety of forest edges and open habitats. The majority of shrike species are found in Europe, Asia and Africa. They are perhaps most famous for the males habit of impaling prey on thorns or between branches to hold them while feeding. Their nests are bulky cups of plants, feathers, hair, sticks and other locally available materials. This is a typical example of a Masked Shrike nest, built by both sexes, and includes rootlets, twigs, plant down, plant stems and moss, and is lined with wool. Shrikes often use wool, hair, or man-made materials in their nests. The Mediterranean population of Masked Shrike are threatened by ongoing degradation of their prefered habitat, but the species is migratory and most of them winter in sub-Saharan Africa and the extreme southwest of the Arabian Peninsula. During migration they are shot in Turkey, the Middle East and Africa, and are locally persecuted in Greece and Syria where they have often been considered birds of ill omen.

Nest size: cup width 56.5 mm (2 ¼ in); cup depth 33.2 mm (1 ¼ in)
Clutch size: 3–7
Collected: nest – 18 May 1909, Troodos Mountains, Cyprus; eggs – May 1906, Cyprus
Conservation: Least Concern

Rook

Corvus frugilegus frugilegus

The family which includes the rook, crows, magpies and jays contains many of the most recognizable and demonstrably intelligent birds in the world. This example of a rook nest was found 19 m (62 ft) up an oak tree next to a road. Rooks usually nest in colonial 'rookeries', ranging from a handful to thousands of nests, built in stands of mature trees, and each tree can have as many as 60 nests. Their nests are bulky structures of twigs and sticks, carefully and clearly lined with roots, leaves and dry grasses. The male brings material to the female who undertakes most of the building work; this nest includes strands of the blue polypropylene cord universally used in agriculture. Researchers at the Universities of Cambridge and Queen Mary, University of London found that Rooks can use, make and modify simple tools. They can even use tools in a sequence to solve a problem. This is especially surprising as Rooks have not been recorded using tools in the wild, yet they rival habitual tools users such as chimpanzees and New Caledonian Crows, *Corvus moneduloides*, when investigated in captivity. The New Caledonian Crow is a species whose sophisticated tool use has also made it renowned as one of the cleverest birds in the world.

Nest size: cup width 210 mm (8 ¼ in); cup depth 80 mm (3 in)
Clutch size: 2–7
Collected: 8 April 2013, under licence Great Glemham, Suffolk by the author
Conservation: Least Concern

Marquesas Monarch

Pomarea mendozae motanensis

The nine *Pomarea* monarch species are an all to familiar example
of the devastation of biodiversity within island ecosystems,
each species being restricted to an island (or islands) in eastern
Polynesia. At least three species have sadly gone extinct within
the last 200 years: the Maupiti Monarch was last seen in 1823,
the Nuku Hiva Monarch was driven to extinction a century later
and the Eiao Monarch was lost before the turn of the 20th century.
Four species are now Critically Endangered and this species, the
Marquesas Monarch, *Pomarea mendozae*, is Endangered. The
endemic subspecies *Pomarea mendozae motanensis* is found on
the tiny uninhabited island of Mohotani, which is now their last refuge.
In 2000 there was around 80–125 pairs with 50 observed in 2007.
The tiny population is thought to be relatively stable but threatened
by continuing habitat degradation from introduced sheep and
predation by introduced cats. A lesser but still significant threat is
the Polynesian rat, introduced by Polynesian explorers before the
arrival of Europeans. This nest is a compact but still quite large
structure made of bark, moss, lichen, twigs, rootlets and plant
down. The nest cup itself is relatively small and carefully lined
with fine plant materials.

Nest size: cup width 50 mm (2 in); cup depth 30 mm (1 in)
Clutch size: 1–2
Collected: April 1975, in a Beach Cherry, *Eugenia reinwardtiana*,
uninhabited island of Mohotani, southern Marquesas Islands
by Jean-Claude Thibault
Conservation: Endangered

White-winged Chough

Corcorax melanorhamphos melanoramphos

There are only two, very different, central and east Australian species in the family Corcoracidae, the White-winged Chough and the Apostlebird, their nesting habits giving them their alternative name, Australian mudnesters. Both species are obligate cooperative breeders, and up to 18 birds within a social group may have all assisted in building this nest, characteristically built on a horizontal bough, probably of a *Eucalyptus* tree. The large conspicuous mud bowl has been built gradually, using pellets of mud in layers, with each layer allowed to dry before the next is added. It is lined with grasses, bark strips and leaves. In this case the nest contained a single clutch of 4 eggs, but several females can all lay in the same nest. This nest is typical in being *c.* 18 cm (7 in) in diameter, but some historical examples were more than 32 cm (13 in) across. Flash droughts and lower-than-normal rates of precipitation, accompanied by abnormally high temperatures, are perhaps a threat to the birds, which need rain to create the mud needed to build their nests.

Nest size: cup width 180 mm (7 in); cup depth 50 mm (2 in)
Clutch size: 3–5
Collected: late 1800s, probably north of the Great Dividing Range, Victoria, southeastern Australia
Conservation: Least Concern

Order _Passeres_
Genus _Corcorax_
Species _melanorhamphus_
Common Name _White winged_
Chough
Locality _Victoria._

Blue-capped Ifrita

Ifrita kowaldi kowaldi

The Blue-capped Ifrita is a true enigma of the New Guinea highlands, and this single species is the only known member of the family Ifritidae. Ifrita are unusual as, like a small number of other New Guinea birds, such as pitohui (see p.116), they have evolved the ability to sequester batrachotoxins from their diet into their feathers and skin. The exact dietary source of the toxins is unclear but New Guinean traditional village naturalists call both ifrita and *Choresine* beetles 'nanisani' – a name that refers to the unusual tingling and numbing sensation to the lips or face caused by contact with either the beetles or ifrita feathers. The birds have evolved resistance to the toxins, but these substances are among the deadliest natural substances known and substantially more toxic than strychnine. In areas of northern New Guinea, some villagers call ifrita 'Slek-Yakt' meaning 'bitter bird'. Local hunters report that eating an ifrita causes a burning sensation stronger than tasting hot chilli peppers. Evolving the ability to use toxins in this way may, therefore, provide some protection against the birds' natural enemies, such as parasites and predators, and even humans. Ifrita nests are built in the forest understorey, and it is likely that the toxins in their feathers and skin rub off onto their deep-cup nests of mosses, lichens, rootlets and leaves, making their nests and eggs one of the few conceivably protected by poison.

Nest size: cup width 40 mm (1½ in); cup depth 55 mm (2¼ in)
Clutch size: 1
Collected: September 1911, Rawlinson Mountains, northeastern Papua New Guinea by Lutheran missionary and naturalist, Christian Keyser
Conservation: Least Concern

Greater Bird-of-Paradise

Paradisaea apoda apoda

When this nest and egg of the Greater Bird-of-Paradise were found in the mid-1920s, the international feather trade was their greatest threat. The first examples of the species to reach Europe probably arrived as trade skins presented to Emperor Charles V of Spain in 1522. By the 1920s, five hundred years of feather trade had developed a preservation method which emphasized their most valuable commodity – the plumes. The shrunken and legless feather rich skins, together with sailors' accounts, led the Spanish court secretary, Maximilianus Transylvanus (*c.* 1485–1538) to conclude: 'a certain most beautiful small bird never rested upon the ground nor upon anything that grew upon it... this bird was born in Paradise ....' Increasingly bizarre myths arose, including the idea that this aerial existence compelled females to lay their eggs in a special cavity on the males back. We now know most of the 42 species of bird-of-paradise build bulky or suspended cup nests with only one, the King Bird-of-Paradise, *Cicinnurus regius*, making nests in holes in trees. This example is the only definitive museum specimen of a Greater Bird-of-Paradise nest. The open cup was built on a horizontal bough supported at both sides by vertical branches, and large leaves formed a base on which stems of epiphytic orchids and vines up to 60 cm (24 in) long were delicately interwoven to make a free-draining, shallow saucer lined with finer stems for the single egg.

Nest size: cup width 120 mm (4 ¾ in); cup depth 35 mm (1 ¼ in)
Clutch size: 1
Collected: October 1925, Waikoa, Aru Islands, eastern Indonesia by Wilfred Frost (1876–1958)
Conservation: Least Concern

Gray-necked Rockfowl

Picathartes oreas

The Gray-necked Rockfowl or 'Kup-akok' meaning 'fowl of the rock', is a restricted range species found in the Cameroon and Gabon Lowlands, and the Cameroon Mountains. These relatively large, strange looking passerine birds are named for their habit of building their nests high on sheltered cliffs or cave walls where they feed on insects, invertebrates and small vertebrates. They also habitually follow army ants, feasting on prey that are trying to escape. The nest, built equally by the male and female together, is a large, heavy cup structure principally made of mud and lined with plant fibres, which is secured to an overhanging rock. They often choose to site the nest where there is a projecting shelf above to protect it from the rain, and the single egg laid is rather long, a glossless creamy white and heavily blotched. They can build new nests on the top of former nests, creating a tiered structure up to 37 cm (14 in) high with distinct layers of earlier nests. This sequential building is probably a result of a lack of available nesting sites. In Nigeria, their preference for nesting in caves and similar sheltered spots, can bring them into direct conflict with man. A significant number of their breeding sites are also used as hunting camps. In 2014 thirty-seven nests (*c.* 95 per cent) recorded in hunting camp locations were seemingly abandoned. The disturbance and direct removal of eggs and fledglings from nests may threaten breeding success in these areas.

Nest size: cup width 140 mm (5½ in); cup depth 60 mm (2¼ in)
Clutch size: 1–3
Collected: Efoulan, southern Cameroon in 1902 by American naturalist George Latimer Bates (1863–1940)
Conservation: Near threatened

Flame Robin

Petroica phoenicea

The *c.* 49 species of small, compact, insectivorous Australasian Robins are found in the forests of Australasia. Most nests are open cups of rootlets, twigs and vine tendrils held together by cobwebs, supported on tree branches or fissures, but they can be placed on the ground close to tree roots, and some resemble a saucer. Flame Robin or Karreet is still abundant throughout the kunanyi/Mount Wellington area in summer. In the mid-1800s ornithologist John Gould wrote: 'It retires to the forests for the purpose of breeding, building its cup-shaped nest in the chink of a tree, in the cleft of a rock, or any similar situation. It is a very familiar species, seeking rather than shunning the presence of man, and readily taking up its abode in his gardens, orchards, and other cultivated grounds. It is to be found in the neighbourhood of Hobart Town at all seasons of the year, and I have even taken its nest from a shelving bank in the streets of the town. The nest, which is thick and warm, is formed of narrow strips and thread-like fibres of soft bark, matted together with cobwebs and sometimes wool, and lined with hair and feathers, or occasionally with fine hair-like grasses.' Today this nest is amongst one of the oldest preserved bird nests in the Museum's collection and one of the oldest from Australia.

Nest size: cup width 40 mm (1½ in); cup depth 30 mm (1 in)
Clutch size: 3
Collected: nest – 15 October 1838, Wellington Park area, near Hobart, Tasmania; eggs – November 1892, Table Cape, Tasmania
Conservation: Least Concern

Petroica phœnicea ?

Specimen marked 175.

Found in all afford

extremity of a felled

tree had in her face

near Mount Wellington

Van Diemen's Land

Oct 15 1838.

Petroica phœnicea

Mt. Wellington

(Van Diemen's Land)

(5.10.1838)   Tasmania

Orange-bellied Flowerpecker

Dicaeum trigonostigma cinereigulare

The flowerpeckers of tropical Asia are woodland and open habitat species. They do not peck flowers exactly, but do flit quickly through forest canopies feeding on fruit and nectar. Relatively little is known of their breeding. The collection of this Orange-bellied Flowerpecker nest and eggs is remarkable as, like many naturalists of the time, disease and 'slow starvation' tormented their collector, the explorer John Whitehead throughout the years he worked in the Philippines. He died of fever less than three years after this nest was colected on the island of Hainan. Thankfully this example was transported safely back for research and was displayed in the museum in South Kensington in the 1890s. Like other known flowerpecker nests it is a beautifully constructed hanging pouch with an entrance on its side, built of mosses, clubmoss and other botanical material held together with spiders' webs. The nest is lined with down from fern fronds and small feathers and delicately suspended from the stem of a large leaf, though the nest itself is small in comparison. The eggs are bluish white, occasionally speckled brown, or sometimes pure white.

Nest size: height 100 mm (4 in); width 60 mm (2¼ in)
Clutch size: 2–3
Collected: nest – 10 August 1896,
Leyte Island in the Visayas group of
islands in the Philippines by
John Whitehead (1860–1899);
eggs – Samar island
Conservation: Least Concern

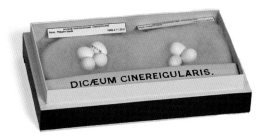

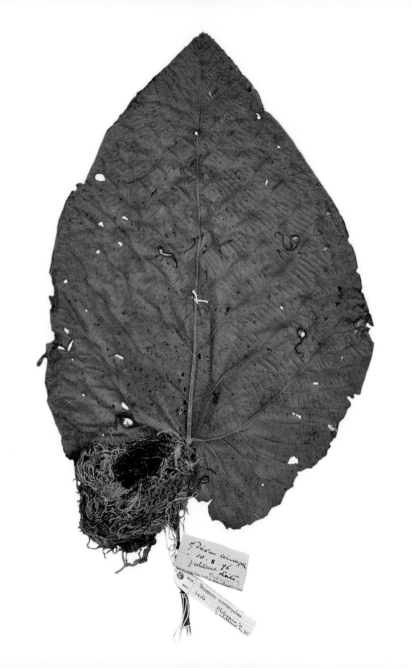

No. 82.
Nest & clutch of two eggs of sunbird
No. 979. Nest hung, 4 feet above
surface of the water, from a bare branch
of an apparently dead shrub standing,
surrounded by swamp-grass, about a
hundred yards from the shore in a swampy
bay near Ambala (Lake Azingo) Gabon.
7 December 1907.

NECTARI...
" NEAR ...ULIGINOSA
GABON (LAKE AZINGO)
7 DEC. 1907
W. J. ANSORGE (C)

Carmelite Sunbird

Chalcomitra fuliginosa aurea

The sunbirds and spiderhunters are ecologically to the Old World as hummingbirds are to the New World. Primarily insectivorous, many of these colourful birds are also highly reliant on the energy-rich nectar they extract from flowers using their specialist bills. Nests are normally dangling, globular structures with a side entrance with trailing vegetation beneath, and this Carmelite Sunbird nest is typical. It is built from leaves, moss and plant fibres and decorated with lichens and lined with down. The label gives more detailed information: 'No. 82. Nest and clutch of two eggs of sunbird No. 979. Nest hung 4 feet above surface of water from a bare branch of an apparently dead shrub standing surrounded by swamps and grass about a hundred yards from the shore of a swampy bay...' To be sure of the identity of the builder, ornithologists at the time routinely shot the parents, then used numbers on labels to cross-refer to the nest, eggs and skins. This may seem callous, but it also ensured that the scientific information gained by collecting was accurate and verifiable. Even today, the only way we can be confident as to which species built a nest is by observing the adults. We can still be sure this nest was built by a Carmelite Sunbird precisely because it can be reliably linked via the collector's numbers to both the skin and eggs.

Nest size: width 70 mm (2 ¾ in); height 190 mm (7 ½ in)
Clutch size: 2
Collected: 7 December 1907, near Anda,
Lake Azingo in Moyen-Ogooué, Gabon
by William J. Ansorge (1850–1913)
Conservation: Least Concern

Dunnock

Prunella modularis modularis

Almost all the members of the accentor family of Europe and Asia are montane birds with one exception – the relatively low-altitude Dunnock, an extraordinarily adaptable bird, equally at home in montane coniferous mixed forest habitats as in lowland hedges, farmland, gardens and parks. This is a characteristic example of their relatively simple cup nest, built of grasses, twigs, moss and rootlets, usually placed in a crevice, on the ground, or in a low bush. The Dunnock has an extremely complex breeding ecology including monogamy (one mate at a time), polygyny (one male with multiple females), polyandry (one female with multiple males) and cooperatively polygynandrous (two or more males that have opted to join forces and defend two or more female territories). They have equally complex sexual behaviours. Often, before intercourse takes place, the female crouches in front of the male, shakes her feathers and lifts her tail to expose her cloaca – the single posterior opening for a bird's digestive, urinary and reproductive tracts. The male responds to this by hopping and pecking at the exposed cloaca, which stimulates the female to eject some of the sperm from any previous mating, thus increasing his chance of paternity.

Nest size: cup width 60 mm (2 ¼ in); cup 40 mm (1 ½ in)
Clutch size: 3–6
Collected: 19 June 1926, near the Birgitten Bach (Pirita) river, Tallin, Estonia by William F. Rosenburg (1868–1957)
Conservation: Least Concern

Prunella m.
modularis.
Nest with 5 eggs.
1947.16.34. Kosih.
Brigittch River.
Tallinn Estonia.
19. 6. 26.
13.9 m. next. Rec. N 143. 108

Village Weaver

Ploceus cucullatus cucullatus

The *c.* 115 weaver species are arguably the most famous nest builders. Their amazingly robust structures are often seen as the epitome of avian architecture, and they have consequently been studied and admired for centuries. It is perhaps therefore not surprising that some of the oldest nests in the Museum's collection are those of weavers. This nest, built by the Village Weaver of sub-Saharan Africa, is our earliest surviving example. Village Weavers are colonial and can build more than 200 nests in a single tree. It is a typically woven, spherical nest with the spout-like entrance facing downwards. This nest would have taken the male around eleven hours to weave using strips torn from reed or palm leaves, with a lining of grasses later added by the female. Recent research has confirmed it was collected during the Niger Expedition of 1841 (officially known as the African Colonization Expedition).

Nest size: width 160 mm (6 ¼ in); height 160 mm (6 ¼ in)
Clutch size: 2–4
Collected: 26 July 1841, near Cape Coast Castle, Ghana by Dr Julius R.T. Vogel (1812–1841)
Conservation: Least Concern

Ibadan Malimbe

Malimbus ibadanensis

Only found in the forests of Ibadan and Ifon Forest Reserve, Nigeria, the Ibaden Malimbe is one of the least known and rarest of all weavers. In June 1965, this extremely rare nest was observed under construction in a small dead tree about 10 m (32 ft) from the ground. Two days later on 27 June the nest chamber was complete, and the male began extending the entrance tunnel, whilst the female lined the egg chamber with materials passed to her by the male. By 5 July laying was inferred and on 26 July young in the nest were being fed by the parents. The collector's attempts to reach the nest to study it further were curtailed after he was stung by Afrotropical wasps. On the 3rd September it was noted that the nest was being immediately reused for a second brood and, despite the continuing attention of wasps, the nest and a single egg was collected for analysis the following day. The nest itself is a typical retort structure, meaning it has a globular nest chamber above and a distinct entrance funnel below. The Ibadan birds were seen to strip Oil Palm leaves whilst building, and tendrils of some climbing plant (possibly *Tietie*) are also incorporated in the nest. Building nests near to wasp colonies may give an extra level of protection from predators such as snakes.

Nest size: nest width 150 mm (6 in); nest height, including entrance: 360 mm (14 in)
Clutch size: 1–2
Collected: 4 September 1965, Ilaro, Ogun State, Nigeria by John Button
Conservation: Endangered

House Sparrow

Passer domesticus biblicus

The Old World sparrows include some of our most familiar birds. Deliberate and accidental introductions, combined with the House Sparrow's flexibility and fondness for man-made structures, have given them an almost worldwide distribution. This nest, perhaps more than any other at the Museum, illustrates their extreme adaptability. On 19 March 2003, a coalition of nations led by the USA opened the second Gulf War against Iraq, known in the UK as Operation Telic. We do not know conclusively which species built this nest, but the nest and eggshell are consistent with the House Sparrow, and they are one of the commonest birds in Iraq. Female sparrows prefer hole nest sites, and they often nest in any available niche on or inside buildings. This nest, however, was built in the exhaust duct of a British Royal Air Force helicopter at the beginning of the conflict in 2003 in Eastern Arabia. House sparrows are remarkably tolerant to disturbance and have even been recorded as nesting on moving vehicles such as cars and small ships. The dominant grass in the construction of this nest is typical of winter-rainfall desert grasses in the area where the British Army's Joint Helicopter Command was based at the time. The nest also includes fig-marigold and goosefoot alongside man-made plastics and cotton thread.

Nest size: width 200 mm (7¾ in); depth 90 mm (3½ in)
Clutch size: 5
Collected: Spring 2003, Eastern Arabia
Conservation: Least Concern

Cape Wagtail

Motacilla capensis capensis

Wagtails and pipits are typically found in open habitats like grasslands, tundra and open woodlands. The name 'wagtail' comes from their ever-present tail bounce as they walk. This Cape Wagtail nest is similar in construction to other wagtail and pipit nests – it is cup-shaped and made up of grasses and other plant material, hair and other materials, including, in this case, string and lined with short hairs and fur. Nests are usually placed in vegetation on the ground and, more rarely, above ground in a bush or tree. Deelfontein, where this nest was found in 1902, had rapidly become a small town, with thousands of patients admitted to the hospital during the Second Boer War, where the collector, Lieutenant Colonel A. T. Sloggett was the medical superintendent. In 1900, ornithologist George Shelly suggested in *The Birds of Africa* that Cape Wagtails often follow cattle or other herbivores, feeding on the insects disturbed and that, near to human habitation, they often select a hole in the wall in which to nest.

Nest size: cup width 50 mm (2 in); cup depth 35 mm (1¼ in)
Clutch size: 1–4
Collected: 4 November 1902, Deelfontein, Great Karoo, South Africa by A.T. Sloggett (1857–1929)
Conservation: Least Concern

Maui 'Alauahio

Paroreomyza montana

The finches, euphonias and Hawaiian honeycreepers are a family of, often colourful, songbirds, found in a range of habitats from arid scrub through to tropical rainforests, volcanic islands to the high alps, and most build relatively simple, open-cup nests. Perhaps one of their most threatened lineages is the extraordinary diversity of Hawaiian honeycreepers, the tribe Drepanini. This is a nest of the Maui 'Alauahio – an Endangered small yellow-green Hawaiian honeycreeper endemic to Maui, and formerly Läna'I where it became extinct around 1937. It is now only found in two forest areas on the east of the island and this nest was found during a research trip to Hosmer Grove, Haleakalā. Pine needles, especially those from fine-needled species such as Mexican weeping pine, and broad, bark strips from Japanese cedar are common components in nests from Hosmer Grove. Another component is pulu, a silky substance obtained from the fibres of the hapu'u pulu tree fern. Climate change is increasing the risk of fires in many areas. The effects of human activity, especially the ongoing degradation of habitat are the greatest threat to their future.

Nest size: cup width 35 mm (1¼ in); cup depth 35 mm (1¼ in)
Clutch size: 2
Collected: 4 July 1995, Hosmer Grove, Haleakalā, Hawai'i
by Paul and Helen Baker
Conservation: Endangered

Snow Bunting

Plectrophenax nivalis nivalis

Most members of the family of longspurs and snow buntings are North American endemics and the majority breed in the Arctic tundra, with only two breeding in the prairies. All build open-cup nests and McKay's Bunting, one of the rarest and most beautiful North American birds, only nest on two small, isolated islands in the Bering Sea. McKay's Bunting evolved from a population of the closely related Snow Bunting that became isolated when sea levels rose at the end of the last ice age. Snow Buntings, by contrast, have a fluctuating circumpolar distribution, breeding largely in the rocky high Arctic tundra across the Nearctic and Palaearctic. The first recorded nest of Snow Bunting in mainland Scotland was found in 1886 and this nest, built by the female, was found in a sheltered, hidden rocky cavity in the Cairngorms around 1,220 m (4,000 ft) above sea level. Nest building is sometimes delayed by late-season snowstorms and this nest was built within 25 m (80 ft) of a big snowfield. Arctic nests, such as those built in Spitsbergen, Norway can often contain more feathers than Scottish nests. This moss and grass nest is barely lined, but Scottish nests have been found that contain as many as 567 ptarmigan feathers, alongside sprays of down, Dotterel and Golden Eagle feathers, red deer hair, sheep's wool and fur from a mountain hare.

Nest size: cup width 58 mm (2¼ in); cup depth 30 mm (1 in)
Clutch size: 4–6
Collected: 11 July 1934, Cairngorms, Scotland by Desmond Nethersole-Thompson (1908–1989)
Conservation: Least Concern

White-naped Brushfinch

Atlapetes albinucha gutturalis

The New World sparrows and their relatives look superficially like their Old World cousins but they are, in fact, quite distantly related. Unlike Old World sparrows, which often nest semi-colonially and build a domed nest or nest in cavities, their New World counterparts, of which the White-naped Brushfinch is one, largely build open-cup nests using twigs, grass and other similar materials. This White-naped Brushfinch nest and eggs from Colombia was collected in the 1870s and is the first known to science. It is a typically open-cup nest built of twigs and dry grasses. Habitat loss threatens 25 species of New World sparrows in the the southern USA, Central America and South America. The Critically Endangered and closely related Antioquia Brush-finch, *Atlapetes blancae*, was only known from three museum specimens collected in 1971, but in 2018 a small population of fewer than 20 individuals were rediscovered in the Colombian Andes. Seventy-three per cent of the natural habitat, in the area where the birds were rediscovered, has already been converted to cattle pastures, and the remaining habitat is equally at risk of being converted to pasture and agricultural land.

Nest size: cup width 55 mm (2 ¼ in); cup depth 40 mm (1 ½ in)
Clutch size: 2–3
Collected: 1870s, Antioquia, left bank of the Cauca River, near Medellin, Andes, Colombia by Colonel Thomas K. Salmon (1840–1878)
Conservation: Least Concern

Black-headed Bunting

Granativora melanocephala

The Old World buntings are open habitat songbirds
found across Europe, Africa and Asia. All typically build
lined, open-cup nests, largely of twigs and grasses, with
most species nesting on or near the ground. This nest
of the Black-headed Bunting was built by the female;
it seems the male contributes very little or nothing to
breeding beyond fertilization, but the male has been
recorded feeding the young. The species is migratory,
with most birds wintering in western India, but Turkey
is well known to be the species breeding stronghold.
There was a notable decrease in breeding numbers
between 1970s and 1990, which is thought to be related
to changes in agricultural practices and the removal
of hedges and shrubs. These changes, together with
heavy pesticide use and other changes in land-use in the
second half of the 20th century, such as the replacement
of olive groves by maize fields, were perhaps the biggest
threat to their future, but it seems their numbers have
now stabilized.

Nest size: cup width 65 mm (2 ½ in); cup depth 35 mm (1 ¼ in)
Clutch size: 4–5
Collected: 18 May 1899, Bournabat (now Bornova),
northeast of Smyrna (now Izmir), Turkey
by Frederick C. Selous (1851–1917)
Conservation: Least Concern

MUS. *Emberiza melanocephala*
BRIT. Bournabat *Asian Turkey*
18. May 1899 *7 c Selous [?]*

Black headed Bunting *(Emberiza)*
Taken near *Bournabat* ——— *may*

Black headed Bunting
Emberiza melanocephala minor
Bournabat *Asia* 1899
May 18

SPINDALIS
WEST IND
1964

B.M.
(N.H.)

Jamaican Spindalis

Spindalis nigricephala

The evolutionary relationship of the stripe-headed tanagers or spindalises has often confused ornithologists. They were considered as Incertae sedis, Latin for 'of uncertain placement', but are now considered by many scientists as a small group of four species endemic to the Caribbean Islands in their own family – the Spindalidae. All build simple, open cups of plant fronds, grasses and rootlets. This nest of the Jamaican Spindalis was one of several found in bunches of bananas exported from Jamaica in the 1960s. The American ornithologist William Earl Dodge Scott noted in 1893 that one of their common names was 'Banana Bird', due to their abundance in the vicinity of any fruit-bearing trees including banana plantations, which increased dramatically in the 20th century. The egg pictured was collected separately but is also from a Jamaican Spindalis.

Nest size: cup width 50 mm (2 in); cup depth 21 mm (¾)
Clutch size: 2–3
Collected: 1960s, from a bunch of bananas, origin Jamaica
Conservation: Least Concern

Streak-backed Oriole

Icterus pustulatus sclateri

The New World blackbird family ranges from the large opopendolas to the smaller American orioles and blackbirds. Many build open-cup nests but the caciques, oropendolas and orioles build long, pendulous baskets of grass or other fibres. This Streak-backed Oriole nest is a typical pensile bag woven from plant fibres and rhizomorphs – the distinctive root-like hyphae created by some fungi. This example, from the mid-1800s, is thought to be one of the first collected for science. It was one of the specimens described in the ground-breaking book *Biologia Centrali-Americana* (1879): 'The materials used by this bird for its nest vary considerably; the structure, however, is the same in all. It is a compact and firmly woven nest, attached at the top to the ends of a bough, its length varying from one to two feet. In some the materials used are fine dried creepers and twigs, with here and there a leaf; in others fibrous roots and the stringy centres of the Maguey leaves, while others are formed exclusively of a species of Tillandsia. All are spherical at the bottom and have a long loophole at the top for an entrance.'

Bag size: width 140 mm (5 ½ in); length 450 mm (17 ¾ in)
Clutch size: 3–4
Collected: 5 May 1860, San Jerónimo, central Guatemala by Robert Owen (1838–1880)
Conservation: Least Concern

Painted Bunting

Passerina ciris ciris

The grosbeaks, buntings and cardinals are in a family of strikingly colourful, New World songbirds, and include some of the most abundant birds of North America such as the Northern Cardinal and Dickcissel. They are primarily fruit and seed-eating species, and the heavy-duty bills of some species often reflect this, whereas some, such as the Lemon-spectacled Tanager of the foothill forests of Ecuador, are insectivorous. We have limited information on some species but, as far we know, they all build open-cup nests, mostly of twigs or stems, and lined with finer materials. This deep-woven cup nest was built by the spectacularly coloured Painted Bunting, whose colloquial name of 'Nonpareil' means 'without equal' and the Painted Bunting is often described as the most beautiful bird in North America. This nest would have been built by the female alone in as little as two days with the lining added after the first egg was laid.

Nest size: cup width 50 mm (2 in); cup depth 40 mm (1½ in)
Clutch size: 3–4
Collected: 13 May 1889, San Antonio, Texas, USA
by William F. Rosenburg (1868–1957)
Conservation: Least Concern

Large Cactus Finch

Geospiza conirostris propinqua

The Genovesa Cactus Finch is one of *c.* 18 species collectively known as 'Darwin's Finches', endemic to the Galápagos Islands, 900 km (560 miles) west of Ecuador. Charles Darwin (1809–1882) famously commented on the divergence of bird species in the Galápagos in *Journal and Remarks* (1839), his first account of his travels round the world on HMS *Beagle,* and later in *On the Origin of Species* (1859). However, it was not until the mid-20th century that British ornithologist David Lack's pioneering study *Darwin's Finches* (1947) convincingly explained that the differences in bill size in each species were adaptations to specific food niches on the islands. This subspecies of Large Cactus Finch is only found on Genovesa Island, in the northeast of the archipelago, where it uses its robust bill to feed on prickly-pear fruits and pulp, flowers and insects. This nest, constructed by the male from grasses and other plants, was collected in 1902 and is now slightly crushed but would have been a spherical structure with its entrance positioned near the top. The blood-sucking nest parasite *Philornis downsi,* introduced to the archipelago in the 1960s probably with imported fruit or poultry, represents one of the most significant threats to the archipelago's land birds but it has thankfully not reached Genovesa Island. Any species with a restricted range is at high risk from introduced pests, diseases and a loss of genetic diversity.

Nest size: width 200 mm (7 ¾ in); overall height 170 mm (6 ¾ in)
Clutch size: 4
Collected: 13 February 1902, Genovesa Island, Galápagos Archipelago by Rollo H. Beck (1870–1950)
Conservation: Vulnerable

MUS. *Trochocercus albonotata*

BRIT.

17.2.1939 Amani, Tang. Terr.
R.E. Moreau [P]

White-tailed Crested-Flycatcher

Elminia albonotata subcaerulea

The small, White-tailed Crested-Flycatcher was long
considered an enigmatic species, with a broken
distribution in the evergreen montane, submontane
and hill forests of East Africa. It is now placed in the
small, recently recognized, family Stenostiridae or fairy
flycatchers that all build open-cup nests. White-tailed
Crested-Flycatcher nests were clearly a favourite of the
British ornithologist Reginald Moreau who collected this
example. In 1933 he noted that: 'the local nests, built
round slender vertical forks a few feet above the ground,
are the most exquisite things of their kind, constructed
wholly of moss, which keeps green all the time the nest
is in use, and are very closely felted.' This example has
also been carefully lined with lichens. As with many
museum examples this would have been a bright, vivid
green when in use. Eighty years in a museum drawer has
inevitably lessened its once vibrant colour scheme.

Nest size: cup width 40 mm (1½ in); cup depth 10 mm (½ in)
Clutch size: 2
Collected: nest – 17 February 1939, Usambara mountains,
Tanzania by Reginald Moreau (1897–1970);
eggs – 19 October 1944, Ndirande, Malawi
Conservation: Least Concern

Blue Tit

Cyanistes caeruleus obscurus

The Blue Tit, like all the *c*. 59 species of tits and chickadees, are largely birds of northern hemisphere forests and all build their nests in cavities. Many tits readily use nest boxes and this abandoned Blue Tit nest, built by the female, is a typical example. Plant fibres mixed with large amounts of moss, small twigs and bast (thin bark strips from dead trees), as well as dried grass, have been layered to make a 7 cm (3 in) deep foundation into which the small nest cup has been formed by the female rubbing and pushing the nest materials with her breast. Once she has formed the cup, she lines it with feathers and animal hair. The cup is usually placed furthest from the entrance to the cavity. Tits can choose almost any cavities for their nests – for example, Blue Tits have been found nesting in wall-mounted steel cigarette bins and Great Tits have nested in letter boxes. A cigarette bin may seem a particularly unusual choice but some birds nesting in cities routinely incorporate cigarette butts into their nests. Butts from smoked cigarettes are poisonous, as they retain substantial amounts of nicotine and other compounds, and the birds may choose to use them as they also act as a parasite repellent.

Nest size: cup width 40 mm (1½ in); cup depth 45 mm (1¾ mm)
Clutch size: 7–13
Collected: April 2020, Briston, north Norfolk, UK
Conservation: Least Concern

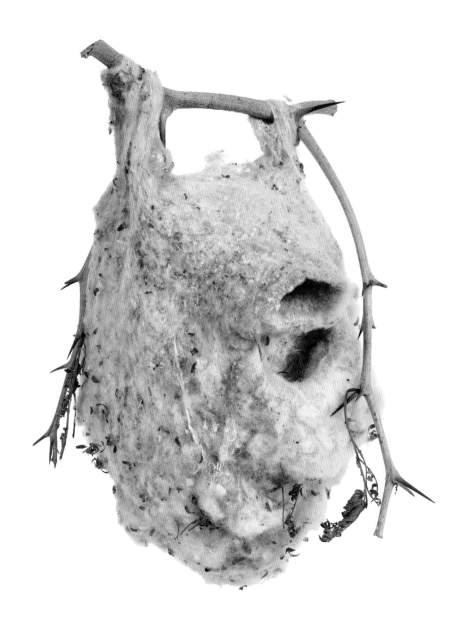

Cape Penduline Tit

Anthoscopus minutus damarensis

Like the weavers, the 11 penduline tit species are also known for their extraordinary nest architecture and this Cape Penduline Tit nest is a superb example. It took both sexes over 20 days to create. The pear-shaped felt bag is woven from soft, downy plant materials felted together with spiders' webs. Over a century after it was made it is still exceptionally strong. It was suspended near the top of a tall thorn-tree over 6 m (20 ft) above the ground near the Cavaco River, Angola. The ornithologist had to cut down the entire tree with an axe to secure the nest for science. Perhaps the most ingenious adaption is the inclusion of a self-closing short tubular entrance, which must be opened by the bird's foot. This entrance is held tightly closed using spiders' webs to protect the five small white eggs. Below this concealed nest-chamber is a deliberately obvious opening to a small false chamber that acts as a decoy to predators like snakes. The edge of the false compartment is reinforced to allow the birds a perch from which they can open the real tubular entrance.

Nest size: width 90 mm (3½ in); height 140 mm (5½ in)
Clutch size: 4–8
Collected: 4 November 1905, near Benguela, Angola by William J. Ansorge (1850–1913)
Conservation: Least Concern

Liben Lark

Heteromirafra archeri sidamoensis

The 93 lark species chiefly build their nests in natural hollows on the ground, lined with grasses and other plant materials over which some Afrotropical species build a woven dome of grass. The remains of this nest, collected during conservation research, represents the heart-breaking story of what will, almost certainly, become the first recorded avian extinction on mainland Africa. These are the remnants of a Critically Endangered Liben Lark nest, collected on the Liben Plain, a small 35 sq km (13 sq miles) area of flat land formerly covered with long grass and scattered *Acacia* bushes east of the town of Negele, southern Ethiopia. The female built the nest from the local, fibrous brown grass woven into the base of a sheltering grass tuft, over which was placed a fragile funnel-shaped, elongate, domed cup. When first found the nest contained three nestlings but it was discovered empty and presumed predated two days later. The plain has been degraded by bush encroachment, permanent settlement and agricultural conversion and, without major intervention, continuing habitat degradation by livestock will almost certainly lead to their rapid extinction. Research in 2009 noted that the survival of both local pastoralism and this bird species

depends on promoting traditional seasonal patterns of grazing, stopping agricultural conversion of grasslands, overturning fire suppression policies and clearing bush. If habitat degradation of the Liben Plains is not reversed rapidly, this is a nesting behaviour we shall never see again.

Box size: length 270 mm (10 ½ in); width 150 mm (6 in); height 100 mm (4 in)
Clutch size: 2–3
Collected: June 2018, Liben Plain, Ethiopia by Dr Nigel Collar, BirdLife International
Conservation: Critically Endangered

Bearded Reedling

Panurus biarmicus biarmicus

The Bearded Reedling is the sole member of the family Panuridae. Synonymous with reedbeds, especially in Eastern Europe, their nests were first figured and described by Dutch naturalist Cornelius Nozeman in 1779. The first nests to be found and scientifically described in Britain were collected from Horsey in Norfolk in 1826. This Norfolk nest is a typical example of their cup-shaped nest, built largely of dead reed blades and water-plants, lined with flowering reed-heads and a few feathers. It would have been built by both sexes, placed near the ground in dense marsh vegetation and held above the water by the coarse reeds, which also provide a canopy above the nest sheltering it from sight. The Bearded Reedling has, over the years, been placed in various families and it is interesting to note that, as far back as 1898, the curator of birds at the British Museum, Richard Bowdler Sharpe, observed that their plumage and nesting, was, in fact, more like the parrotbills of South Asia – birds we still know little about. Now we think they are related to the larks (Alaudidae) and equally engmatic nicators (Nicatoridae). Their eggs differ from all other British birds – they are glossy white with minute specks and short, irregular lines of reddish-brown. Their UK numbers declined in the 20th century, and they often do not cope well with long, cold winters. In recent decades they have increased in both numbers and range, and they may becoming less susceptible or benefiting from the milder winters resulting from climate change.

Nest size: cup width 50 mm (2 in); cup depth 30 mm (1 in)
Clutch size: 3–11
Collected: 10 May 1907, Hickling Broads, Norfolk, UK
Conservation: Least Concern

Long-billed Crombec

Sylvietta rufescens ansorgei

The crombecs, longbills and allies are African, warbler-like, birds recently recognized as a separate family. Little is known of the breeding of many of these so-called African warblers, for example the Short-billed Crombec, *Sylvietta philippae,* of Somalia and Ethiopia, but those that have been studied build open-cup nests made of grasses and fine twigs. The nests of crombecs are especially deep cups, often described as purse-, or bottle-shaped. The name 'crombec' (Dutch for 'curved bill'), was first recorded, and rather exaggeratingly illustrated by naturalist François Levaillant in 1802. Their name might be considered a slight misnomer given their relatively straight bill but the races of Long-billed Crombec do vary in depth of coloration and bill length. Many African warblers, especially the crombecs, use large amounts of spiders' webs to hold the nest together, to attach it to the tree or bush and to decorate the exterior. The Long-billed Crombec is found throughout southern Africa and this nest is a typical example of their purse-shaped nests of plant fibres, grass leaves, bark-strips and lichen, all held together with copious quantities of arthropod silk. Spiders' webs were also used to attach it to a thornbush where it was suspended less than a metre above the ground.

Nest size: width 30 mm (1 in); depth 40 mm (1½ in)
Clutch size: 1–3
Collected: 3 November 1905, near the Cavaco River, Benguela, Angola by William J. Ansorge (1850–1913)
Conservation: Least Concern

SYLVIETTA ANSORGEI
S CAVACO RIVER (BENGUELLA
S TOWN) , ANGOLA
3 NOV. 1905.   W. J. ANSORGE (C)

BRIT. MUS. (N.H.)

Nº 15

Nest with clutch of 3 eggs of near
Nº 569. Nest was [unfinished] in
Thornbush about 3 feet above
ground. Cavaco river (Suimod of
Benguella Town) Angola.
Nov. 3.1905.   W. J. Ansorge.

C. aridula
Booksmhout.
Ad. H. Lynes
12 Dec.
He/f
Cat. 79 E 28·11·8
40·44

C·79
28·11·8
43

C·79
28·11·8

Desert Cisticola

Cisticola aridulus kalahari

Cisticolas are small, primarily insectivorous, long-tailed, warbler-like birds of Africa, Asia and Australia. Most build ball-shaped nests and this Desert Cisticola nest was collected during one of the most comprehensive and ground-breaking studies of a single avian genus ever undertaken. The 51 Cisticola species can vary markedly in their size, songs and ecology but can also look confusingly similar. Consequently at the beginning of the 20th century there was a range of scientific questions about their taxonomy and biology and in December 1925 Admiral Hubert Lynes, also an ornithologist, took up the challenge. He began five years of meticulous research across Africa, assisted by B. B. Osmaston and supported by a large contingent of African naturalists. He wanted to find as many species of *Cisticola* in their nesting season as possible. The result was a massive collection of research specimens which ultimately resulted in the publication of his ground-breaking *Review of the Genus Cisticola* published as a special volume of *The Ibis* in 1930. It remains a stunning piece of work and it made him internationally famous as an ornithologist. His study classified three types of nests in the family: 'soda-bottle', 'tailor' and this nest which he dissected and figured to illustrate a typical 'ball' nest, elliptical in shape, with a roof and side-top entrance-hole. It was built in 4–5 days of dry grass bound with spiders' webs. Lynes spent many hours watching the birds build this nest and later the female adding fine plant down to line the nest once the four eggs were laid.

Nest size: width 45 mm (1 ¾ in); length 120 mm (4 ¾ in)
Clutch size: 2–5
Collected: 12 December 1926, near Pretoria, South Africa
by Rear Admiral Hubert Lynes (1874–1942)
Conservation: Least Concern

Rusty Thicketbird

Megalurulus rubiginosus

The bush warbler family are almost all secretive, dull plumaged birds of dense undergrowth which, as far as we know, build deep-cup, sometimes domed, nests. They are difficult to study due to their often impenetrable habitat of dense undergrowth and marshes. This bush warbler, the Rusty Thicketbird, is only found in the lowlands of the island of New Britain, Papua New Guinea and is one of the most poorly known. The collector of this extremely rare nest and two red-speckled eggs provided very limited information about it, simply indicating: 'this brown, very rare Timaliid, builds a loose-leaf nest on the ground.' In 1880 the German naturalist Theodor Kleinschmidt was the first western scientist to collect specimens for science and his description of its habits remains one of the few published accounts: 'Lives on the ground and runs with head projecting forwards like a Quail. When in captivity it retired at night into a bundle of grass placed in the corner of its cage on the ground to sleep. Here, suddenly expanding its long dorsal feathers, sinking its rounded wings, and drawing in its head, it looked like a loose round bundle of brown grass-stalks. Food grasshoppers. Iris bright grey, with a light-brown tinge; bill dark horn-colour above, almost black, beneath brighter; legs, feet, and claws dark horn-colour. Native name Talberara. Breeds in November and December and said to lay in a hollow in the ground without any nest.' The true nature of its nest building was not recognized until this specimen was collected 48 years later.

Nest size: cup width 60 mm (2¼ in); cup depth 30 mm (1 in)
Clutch size: 2
Collected: May 1928, Bitokara in West New Britain Province, Papua New Guinea by Otto Meyer
Conservation: Least Concern

Ortigocichla rubiginosa

oriatess New Britain Archp.
.5 1928
Rothschild Beq.

Laysan Millerbird

Acrocephalus familiaris familiaris

Perhaps most famous for their songs, the reed warblers and their relatives live in a variety of habitats from marshes to forests across the Old World and Australasia. Many of the Pacific islands host endemic species of reed warbler, which evolved through successive waves of colonization over several million years. All species usually build cup nests constructed of grasses and reeds and lined with finer material, placed in reeds, shrubs or trees. The Laysan Millerbird is a reed warbler that was once plentiful and very tame on Laysan Island in the Hawaiian Archipelago. They reportedly built their nests in the tall bunchgrass (kāwelu) surrounding the interior salt lake on the island. They are known as Millerbirds as they fed on the large white moths known as 'Millers' on the islands, but the introduction of rabbits devastated the moths' habitat. It was speculated in 1963 that one of the major factors influencing the extinction of two of Laysan's endemic birds, the Laysan Honeyeater and the Laysan Millerbird, was the disappearance of several of the endemic 'Miller' moths that formed their major food source including the Laysan noctuid moth, *Agrotis laysanensis*. The deep nest cup, formed from dried grass stems, rootlets and twigs, almost completely obscured by feathers from the Laysan Albatross, *Phoebastria immutabilis*, was almost certainly built by both sexes working cooperatively.

Nest size: cup width 40 mm (1½ in); cup depth 50 mm (2 in)
Clutch size: 2–3
Collected: 27 May 1896, Laysan Island, Hawaiian Archipelago by Henry C. Palmer (1866–1920)
Conservation: Extinct

Welcome Swallow

Hirundo neoxena neoxena

Swallows are highly recognizable and specialized aerial insectivores. Some species nest in burrows in sandy soils, others adopt cavities and many, like this Welcome Swallow of Australia and New Zealand, construct nests of mud. This example was found on a stable rafter, and sent to the ornithologist John Gould in London in the spring of 1862 to help him write his *Handbook to the Birds of Australia* in which he wrote: 'The natural breeding-places of this bird are the deep clefts of rocks and dark caverns, but since the colonization of Australia it has in a remarkable degree imitated its European prototype, by selecting for the site of its nest the smoky chimneys, the chambers of mills and out-houses, or the corner of a shady verandah; the nest is also similarly constructed, being open at the top, formed of mud or clay, intermingled with grass or straw to bind it firmly together, and lined first with a layer of fine grasses, and then with feathers. The shape of the nest depends upon the situation in which it is built, but it generally assumes a rounded contour in front.' Nests are constructed by both sexes either singly, in loose groups or colonially, with up to as many as 500 birds building in one site. Each nest can take anything from 6–24 days to build, with most of the building activity taking place in the early morning.

Nest size: cup width 90 mm (3 ½ in); cup depth 50 mm (2 in)
Clutch size: 2–7
Collected: nest - 3 October 1861, Collingrove Homestead, southeast of Angaston, Barossa Valley, South Australia by George F. Angas (1822–1886); eggs - 12 September 1882 from a different nest in Victoria, South Australia
Conservation: Least Concern

Styan's or Taiwanese light-vented Bulbul

Pycnonotus taivanus formosae

This Taiwanese light-vented Bulbul (also known as Styan's Bulbul) nest and eggs is typical of the open-cup nests made by most bulbuls. Found in Taipei in 1896, its collectors packed it in a handmade paper container for transport and remarkably it is still held in its original packaging today; and one of the three brightly speckled eggs has never been unwrapped. The Latin name *formosae* comes from the Portuguese 'Ilha Formosa' meaning 'beautiful island', so named when Portuguese explorers sighted the island around 1542. The subspecies of Light-vented Bulbul found on Taiwan was only scientifically described in 1910 using specimens from the same collector. Nests in Taiwan are often made of swordgrass flower spikes and leaves and lined with stripped flower spikes. However, this nest is largely constructed of twigs and bamboo leaves and was found in a small group of bamboo 3 m (10 ft) above the ground.

Nest size: cup width 70 mm (2 ¾ in); cup depth 65 mm (2 ½ in)
Clutch size: 3–4
Collected: 2 June 1896, Taipei by Japanese naturalists working with the British natural historian Alan Owston
Conservation: Vulnerable

No. 10
Loc. name. Pi-loh
Position of nest. In bamboo copse
                    10 ft. above ground

Loc. Taipeh. Formosa
    Date. 2.6.96

10 王玉

Gray-cheeked Leaf Warbler

Seicercus poliogenys

The leaf warblers are all tiny songbirds that forage restlessly in dense foliage for insects. The Gray-cheeked Warbler is a small leaf warbler found in the biodiversity-rich eastern Himalaya through to Thailand and Vietnam. Like most of its family it usually builds a ball nest of moss and grasses, and these are the rare remnants of a moss nest and five eggs. It is unclear as to whether this rather solid, cup-shaped nest is correctly identified or complete, but similar nests were found among the moss growing on the stem of a small tree in Sikkim, northeastern India by the Scottish gardener and botanist James Gammie (1839–1924) in the late 1800s, each nest lined with moss and rootlets and a few leaves. Their breeding is still little known and barely studied. The Himalayan population, where this nest was found, seem to have a more complex song than those found in China and Vietnam, and further research on their genetics, breeding and wider ecology may yet show them to be a distinct species from those in the east of their range.

Nest size: cup width 70 mm (2 ¾ in); cup depth 35 mm (1 ¼ in)
Clutch size: 4–5
Collected: 15 May 1920, probably found on or near the ground in the lush undergrowth of the foothills of the Himalaya at Gopaldhara, West Bengal, India
by Herbert Stevens (1877–1964)
Conservation: Least Concern

Rufous-faced Warbler

Abroscopus albogularis fulvifacies

The bush warblers are all shy, skulking birds of dense forests in Afro-Eurasia. Rufous-faced Warblers habitually build their nests in natural holes and split or broken bamboo. Both these nests are fascinating early examples of man-made nest holes. The larger piece of bamboo contains a small, 5 cm (2 in) wide, nest found on 4 May 1898 in which the birds were observed nesting in April. An enterprising Chinese boy realized that he could entice the birds to nest in an old piece of bamboo if he cut out a section and placed it just below his home. He then sold both sets of nests and eggs to the pioneering Irish naturalist John La Touche. The larger nest, on the left, is built on a deep 13 cm (5 in) base of bamboo leaves placed upright by the birds in the stem and lined with coir-fibre. The nest on the right has been opened entirely to show its construction, but had likewise originally been built in an artificially made bamboo nest box.

Bamboo size: width 85 mm (3¼ in)
Clutch size: 3–5
Collected: 1898, Kuatun, northwestern Fujian, China
by a young Chinese naturalist working with
John La Touche (1844–1921)
Conservation: Least Concern

Long-tailed Tit

Aegithalos caudatus trivirgatus

The Long-tailed Tits are named for their distinctively long tails, often at odds with their otherwise petite size. Most build characteristically globular or pendant nests of moss and lichens felted together by spiders' webs and feathers from other birds. The 'original' Long-tailed Tit, first described by Carl Linnaeus in 1758, is now split into two distinct groups: the 'europeaeus' groups of subspecies and the 'trivirgatus' subspecies from Korea and Japan. This example is a typical nest. It would have taken both sexes up to 33 days to complete this compact, oval ball of moss, held together with cobwebs. Each nest is decorated with up to *c.* 3,000 individual pieces of lichen, each cemented in place with spiders' webs. The entrance hole is placed on the side and leads to a cavity lined with as many as 2,680 small feathers. This example is still held in the carefully made cardboard container made by the collector to transport it back to London.

Nest size: width 85 mm (3 ¼ in); height 130 mm (5 in)
Clutch size: 6–15
Collected: 7 April 1897, near the town of Gotemba, southeastern flank of Mount Fuji, Japan
Conservation: Least Concern

O.C.
4425
Acredula trivirgata
nest in *mimosa Columba*
Jananura
Apri. 7. 97. Cont 2 6 Egge

...lus caudalis trivirgatus
Gotemba Japan
Rothschild Beq.

MUS.
BRIT.

Sylvia a. atricapilla

Manningtree Essex
16. 6. 09

Eurasian Blackcap

Sylvia atricapilla atricapilla

The blackcap has long been lauded as one of Europe's finest songbirds and historically they were also known as the 'Mock Nightingale'. This nest was found in an Elder roughly a metre from the ground in Essex, UK in 1909. It is one of three nests built by the same pair in the same tree that year. In some areas of Europe, blackcap will usually have two broods, one in spring and the other in autumn. The collection of this nest in mid-June may have stimulated the birds to make another nesting attempt. The delicately structured open-cup nest is like other sylviid warblers, carefully built of twigs and rootlets and lined with grasses. The clutch size varies with latitude, altitude and the season. First clutches can number as many as six eggs, but later clutches are often smaller. Their eggs were beautifully described by zoologist William Yarrell in 1843 as: 'pale greenish white, mottled with light brown and ash colour, with a few spots and streaks of dark brown.' Interestingly, the collector of this nest noted on the label that the last clutch of three eggs were white. The exact causes of changes in eggshell coloration between a sequence of eggs or clutches are not well understood but both are probably related to health or stress at the time of laying.

Nest size: cup width 50 mm (2 in); cup depth 40 mm (1½ in)
Clutch size: 2–7
Collected: 16 June 1909, Manningtree, Essex probably by W. B. Nicholl
Conservation: Least Concern

Golden White-eye

Cleptornis marchei

The Golden White-eye is only found on the islands of Saipan and Aguijan in the northern Mariana Islands. It is one of the most striking and unmistakeable of the white-eyes. Like other white-eyes they build open-cup nests, hung between the forked ends of branches. The naturalist Ernst Hartert wrote: 'A nest was found on July 7th in a 'Rakiti' tree. It hangs in the fork of a thin branch, just like the nest of a golden Oriole, at the end concealed by the long oval laurel-like leaves of the 'Rakiti.' The sides of the nest are not very tightly woven and consist of roots, grasses, etc., outside beautifully ornamented with small leaves and the silk of light green cocoons.' The lime green silk comes from the cocoons of silk moths. Whilst the evanescent green of the plants has faded, the silk is still as vibrant today as the day it was selected and incorporated into their nest. The use of green silk from cocoons is also seen in nests built by the extinct Bridled White-eye and the extinct Micronesian Myzomela from Guåhan (Guam). Both were extirpated by the invasive brown tree snake, native to Australia and Papau New Guinea, which was accidentally introduced in imported cargo, and first detected on Guåhan in the 1950s. In 2016 the snakes were also reported on Saipan. Golden White-eyes are already severely threatened

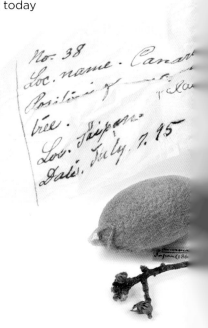

by habitat loss and if these snakes become established on Saipan, it would lead to a devastating decline in all the islands' birds, including the Golden White-eye.

Nest size: cup width 50 mm (2 in); cup depth 50 mm (2 in)
Clutch size: 2
Collected: 7 July 1895, Saipan by Alan Owston (1853–1915)
Conservation: Endangered

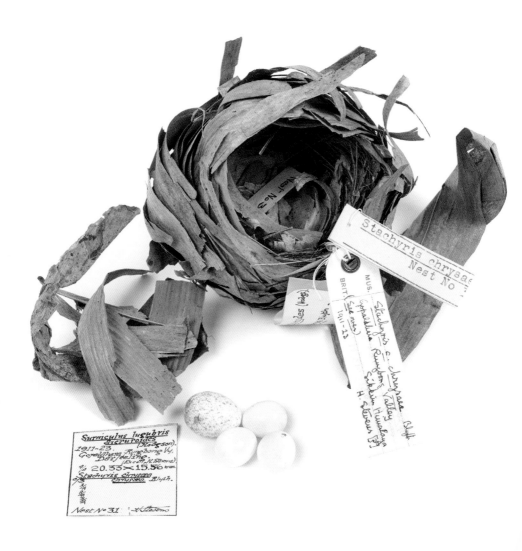

Stachyris chrysae
Nest No.

Nest No.2

MUS.
BRIT.
1911-23

Stachyris c.
chrysaea.......
Rungbong Valley
Sikkim Himalaya
H. Stevens [?]

Surniculus lugubris
dicruroides
(Hodgson).
1911-23.
Gorabhang Rungbong Vy.
Darjeeling
(Excott./H.Stevens)
½ 20.33×15.56 mm.
Stachyris chrysaea
chrysaea Blyth.
Nest No 31 . H.Stevens

Golden Babbler

Cyanoderma chrysaeum chrysaeum

The Golden Babbler is a distinctive small, tree babbler of evergreen forests, bamboo and secondary forest. They typically build a domed nest with an entrance near the top. This example is made of dried bamboo and lined with rootlets. Three white eggs were laid by the female babbler, but a fourth egg was also found in the nest. This larger, conspicuously grey-white egg sparsely speckled with brown, was laid by a brood parasite, and the size, colour and label implicate the Fork-tailed Drongo-Cuckoo as the culprit. Relatively little is known of this cuckoo's breeding ecology but, like other obligate brood parasites, they must lay their eggs in the nests of other species. The Golden Babbler is not a noted host of this cuckoo but, if the babbler failed to recognize and remove the parasite's egg, it would have ejected the host's eggs and chicks soon after hatching.

Nest size: cup width 45 mm (1¾ in); cup depth 45 mm (1¾ in)
Clutch size: 3–4
Collected: early 1900s, Gopaldhara, West Bengal
by Herbert Stevens
Conservation: Least Concern

Scaly-breasted Illadopsis

Illadopsis albipectus

The Scaly-breasted Illadopsis is a small ground-babbler found in Central and East Africa. This is the only example of their nest that has been deposited in a museum and scientifically described, and was one of eight nests found as part of PhD research on their behaviour and habitat. Like many ground-babbler nests it is a small, loose cup of decomposing leaves, twigs, rootlets, and moss, and lined with finer materials. Two dissimilar eggs, which differ in size, pigmentation and shape, were found in the nest, and it is possible that one of these was laid by a brood parasite. The only way to research this conclusively would be if DNA could be successfully extracted from the eggs and compared with known sequences, to reveal the species that laid both eggs.

Nest size: cup width 60 mm (2¼ in); cup depth 40 mm (1½ in)
Clutch size: 2
Collected: 4 May 1999, Budongo Foreset Reserve, western Uganda by Jeremy Lindsell
Conservation: Least Concern

Red-billed Leiothrix

Leiothrix lutea calipyga

The Red-billed Leiothrix were historically popular cage birds in China and in 1868 the surgeon and naturalist Cuthbert Collingwood tried, unsuccessfully, to take live examples of the 'Pekin Robin', back to the UK. They were commonly imported as cage birds up until 2005, when the European Union banned further imports. However, a small number have escaped and are thought to be breeding in England – the warming climate and garden bird-feeding might help them establish across Europe. In the early 1900s they were introduced to Hawai'i and less than 20 years later they were one of the commonest birds on the island, and possibly a factor in the decline and extinction of several endemic Hawaiian forest birds. These green and yellow babblers are habitually found in open broadleaf, pine and mixed forests, and are sometimes common in the tea plantations of the eastern Himalaya, which partially explains this large collection of nests made of grasses, leaves and rootlets. They were all collected by naturalist Herbert Stevens who took over as manager of the Gopaldhara Tea Estate in Darjeeling, West Bengal for 10 years from 1911. Overall, he collected more than 1,200 nests of more than a hundred species. All nests are botanical time capsules and potential sources of genetic information that might be used in future to address countless ecological questions, so this extraordinary wealth of nests in the Museum represents an exceptional and unique opportunity to research the breeding ecology of the birds of northeastern India.

Box size: width 220 mm (8¾ in); height 60 mm (2¼ in); length: 420 mm (16½ in);
Nest size: cup width 45 mm (1¾ in); cup depth 35 mm (1¼ in)
Clutch size: 3–5
Collected: northeast India by Herbert Stevens
Conservation: Least Concern

MUS.   *Regulus madeirensis*

BRIT

Madeira
Rothschild Bequest

Madeira Firecrest

Regulus madeirensis

The Madeira Firecrest was found over most of the island of Madeira, especially in the evergreen subtropical Laurel Forest (Laurisilva) that once blanketed the island. Whilst the species is not considered at risk, the gradual replacement of the indigenous laurel forest by introduced *Eucalyptus* plantations is a concern. Thankfully much of the remaining Laurisilva is within the Parque Natural da Madeira (Madeira Natural Park), which protects the largest surviving area of primary forest. The firecrests are absent where the introduced *Eucalyptus* has spread extensively on the south slopes of Madeira, displacing the native trees and plants. The Madeira Firecrest is the smallest bird in Europe but conversely builds a relatively large nest with a dry weight of over 30 g (1 oz), over 4 times the mass of the tiny 7 g (¼ oz) bird. Like the other firecrests, goldcrests and kinglets it builds a deep cup-shaped, almost globular, nest with a small, restricted opening at the top. This nest is made principally of moss, and some fine twigs felted together with spiders' webs, but it lacks an inner cushion layer with few, if any, feathers and little or no outer covering of lichens compared with nests of Common Firecrest and the closely related Goldcrest (whose nests are often heavily decorated with lichens).

Nest size: cup width 40 mm (1½ in); cup depth 40 mm (1½ in)
Clutch size: *c.* 6–13
Collected: *c.* May 1903, Madeira by the Catholic priest and pioneer of Madeiran natural history Ernst Johann Schmitz
Conservation: Least Concern

Bohemian Waxwing

Bombycilla garrulus garrulus

The Bohemian Waxwing is familiar to most as a beautiful and enchanting winter visitor across the northern hemisphere and can arrive in large numbers or irruptions – 34,000 arrived in one region of southwest Germany during the winter of 2004–2005. The waxwings reliance on berries means they often eat naturally fermented fruit long past their prime, occasionally getting thoroughly intoxicated in the process. The relatively large livers of waxwings, and other species that rely on berries to get through winter, may help the birds handle alcohol. They nest in open coniferous forest, such as the taiga of central Alaska and other boreal forests globally. This specimen is a typical small 6 cm (2 ½ in) diameter cup built of pine twigs, fine plant fibres and camouflaged with mosses and lichens, the untidy, somewhat scruffy masses of external mosses and plant fibres helping to conceal the nest. Both males and females gather nesting material with the female doing most of the actual building and shaping. Four to five light blue-grey eggs sparsely spotted with dark blotches were laid in the nest. Examination of the nest suggests it was probably built on a horizontal branch near the main trunk.

Nest size: cup width 60 mm (2 ½ in); cup depth 25 mm (1 in)
Clutch size: 4–6
Collected: 23 June 1892, Kvikkjokk, northern Sweden
Conservation: Least Concern

Hypocolius

Hypocolius ampelinus

The *Hypocolius* is the only member of the family
Hypocoliidae; this distinctive, long-tailed and sleek
Middle Eastern bird is related to the waxwings. Naturalist
Walter D. Cumming (1858–1924) of the McMahon Museum
in Quetta, Pakistan was the first to study their breeding
in detail in the 1880s at the Al-Faw peninsula in southern
Iraq. His detailed notes and specimens confirmed each
nest was built in 3–4 days and he and local collectors
found and documented dozens of examples. The deep
nest cup constructed of twigs, plant down and wool
was found in a loose colony with other breeding pairs.
Only one glossy, leaden-white egg remains, but the
usual clutch size is 3–5 eggs. The species is considered
reasonably common and of Least Concern, but their
actual population size and precise range are still poorly
known so, like many species, assessing their true
conservation status and risk is challenging. The small
patches of riverine forest where they often breed are still
threatened. By the 1950s many of the riverine forests of
the Iraqi alluvial plains had been lost through cultivation.

Nest size: cup width 75 mm (3 in); cup depth 60 mm (2 ¼ in)
Clutch size: 3–5
Collected: 16 May 1921, near Baghdad, central Iraq
Conservation: Least Concern

Certhia discolor discolor Blyth.
c/4   Nest No 235.   26.4.1919

MUS.
BRIT.
Certhia d. discolor Blyth
Gopaldhara
Rungbong Valley c/x Darjeeling
26. 4. 1919
H. Stevens [P]

Sikkim Treecreeper

Certhia discolor

Virtually nothing is published on the breeding of the Sikkim Treecreeper of the eastern Himalaya and it has only recently been recognized as a separate species based on vocal and genetic differences. It was thought that the breeding season of the Sikkim Treecreeper was likely to be March to May in the Himalaya and this nest, collected in April 1919 and somewhat overlooked by science for a century, confirms that assumption. All treecreepers are thought to construct a pad nest of fibre, moss and a few roots, occasionally lined with a few feathers, in crevices between bark and the underlying tree trunk (or suitable holes made by woodpeckers). This nest is a pad of loose bark fragments and twigs onto which a further cup of plant down and fine plant materials has been arranged, with a clutch of four white eggs heavily spotted with red. The original set of eggs are missing and may have been part of a theft in the late 1970s. The set of eggs shown are catalogued as being laid by the same species, collected in the East Khasi Hills district of Assam from unconfirmed nests that had thick fur linings from either the Bamboo-rat or shrew.

Pad size: width 90 mm (3 ½ in); 35 mm (1 ¼ in)
Clutch size: *c.* 3–4
Collected: 26 April 1919, Gopaldhara, Rungbong Valley, Darjeeling, India
Conservation: Least Concern

Corsican Nuthatch

Sitta whiteheadi

The Corsican Nuthatch or Pichiu is in a family of small, short-tailed birds all of which are well-adapted to their life of foraging up and down tree trunks and rock-walls. The species was only formally discovered in June 1883 by the naturalist John Whitehead (after whom it is named) whilst he was searching for an eagle's nest. The following year he returned to the same mountain forests of Corsica and during 11 days of fieldwork he finally discovered nine nests in mid-May. Many were inaccessibly high in holes 20–30 m (65–98 ft) from the ground, in dead and decaying pine trees. However, he did manage to access a few nests, and this is some of the nest material he collected from inside a cavity in one of those decaying Corsican pines in 1884. Both sexes would have excavated the hole into which this crude foundation of moss, plant-fibres, woodchips and feathers was placed. Whitehead himself realized that the species was uncommon and restricted to a few inland mountain ridges on Corsica. Determined not to risk its future, he never divulged the exact locality where he found them when he formally described the species, and Whitehead took the secret to his grave in 1899. They were not seen again by scientists until the German ornithologist Alexander Koenig found them at the Vizzavona Forest during the spring of 1896.

Nest size: width 16.5 mm (½ in); 100 mm (4 in)
Clutch size: *c.* 5–6
Collected: 30 May 1884, Corsica
Conservation: Vulnerable

Sitta whiteheadi.
Corsica
J. Whitehead [P.]

Sitta whiteheadii.   B.M. Reg
                      J. Whitehead N.281.

Marsh Wren

Cistothorus palustris palustris

The Marsh Wren builds a domed nest often made of sedges and grass with a neat side entrance. This example was collected with the supporting reeds still woven directly into the nest. William Earl Dodge Scott, who obtained this nest whilst collecting for the Museum of Biology at Princeton University, also described the males intriguing habit of building multiple 'dummy' nests: 'At one time in a small marsh, not more than forty feet long and some twenty-five wide, and only occupied by a single pair of birds, I found eight new nests. One of these contained five fresh eggs, and the others were to all appearance the result of the efforts of the male bird. I visited the place when it contained but two nests, and the others were built in the succeeding ten days. They were none of them ever used, save the one that contained five eggs, for breeding in.' Males can build more than 22 nests in a season and each nest can take up to three days to complete. Building several nests could provide decoys for predators and indicate a male's strength, stamina and quality of territory. However, research in the 1990s did not establish exactly why the 'dummy nests' are built and it remains an ornithological enigma.

Nest size: width 130 mm (5 in)
Clutch size: 4–6
Collected: nest – 10 June 1877, New Jersey, USA
by William Earl Dodge Scott (1852–1910);
eggs – 28 June 1877, same location
Conservation: Least Concern

Blue-gray Gnatcatcher

Polioptila caerulea caerulea

The gnatcatchers are tiny insectivorous birds found in the New World. The Blue-gray Gnatcatcher was memorably described by the pioneering American ornithologist Frank Chapman as 'a bird of strong character' and it is the only gnatcatcher found in the colder temperate regions, breeding from Ontario, Canada, south to El Salvador and eastward from California to Maine in the USA. They are one of the earliest breeding insectivorous songbirds with nest building in California beginning in mid-April, and nesting varies by around one month latitudinally. This nest was found in a tree about 12 m (40 ft) from the ground on a hillside in dense woods. The male and female would have contributed to its building. The high-walled cup is typical of this species and made of tendrils of plant fibres, bark strips and fine grasses held together by spiders' webs, with the outside carefully camouflaged using crustose lichens and some feathers. Each concentric layer has been built up progressively using ever thinner materials, with the finest and softest comprising the innermost lining. Four bluish-white eggs covered with small spots were laid in the nest. They are regularly parasitized by the Brown-headed Cowbird. As they have no capacity to eject or puncture cowbird eggs this could be contributing to the regional population declines so, for example, in California they have now been lost in some areas and brood-parasitism is the prime suspect.

Nest size: width 30 mm (1 in); cup depth 50 mm (2 in)
Clutch size: 4
Collected: 18 May 1882, Brookville, Indiana, USA
Conservation: Least Concern

San Cristóbal Mockingbird

Mimus melanotis

Mockingbirds are common, open-habitat birds in the Americas that typically build ungainly, open-cup nests of twigs, rootlets and grasses. This nest and eggs belong to the endemic Mockingbird of San Cristóbal Island, the easternmost island in the Galápagos, and one of the geologically oldest Islands in the famous archipelago. San Cristóbal (also known as Chatham) Island was the first Galápagos island visited by Charles Darwin in 1835. Seventy-six years later, the ornithologist Rollo Beck found and collected this nest in March 1901. Until recently they were considered Endangered, but the island's population of mockingbirds has stabilized in recent decades. However, the invasive parasitic fly, *Philornis downsi,* is an ongoing threat to all the avifauna of the Galápagos. The parasite is native to mainland South America and probably introduced to the Galápagos from mainland Ecuador in the mid-20th century. The fly's larvae feed on the nestlings of at least 18 endemic and native birds in the archipelago. Several species of bird are thought to include green plant material after nest building to reduce parasite infestation, but we still cannot conclusively explain the evolutionary cause for birds adding fresh green aromatic herbs to their nests and it is a behaviour which needs research.

Nest size: cup width 70 mm (2 ¾ in); cup depth 50 mm (2 in)
Clutch size: 2–5
Collected: 15 March 1901, San Cristóbal Island, easternmost island of the Galápagos
Conservation: Near Threatened

Norfolk Starling

Aplonis fusca fusca

The *Aplonis* starlings are a group of *c.* 25 closely related species restricted to islands in Indonesia and Oceania. The Norfolk Starling was only found on Norfolk Island, a remote location east of Australia. Norfolk Island was once covered with dense subtropical rainforest dominated by the endemic Norfolk Island pine *Araucaria heterophylla*, together with palms, hardwoods and fern forests. Less than 150 years after the first European, Captain James Cook, set foot on Norfolk in October 1774, the dual impact of widescale deforestation, habitat destruction and persecution led to their demise on Norfolk Island. Their gregarious preference for fruit crops like bananas meant that they were vigorously hunted, and the last bird was seen in 1923. The little bird had the habit of nesting in holes in trees or ferns and in 1909 the Australian naturalist Arthur Francis Basset Hull described their nests as 'a slight open structure of small twigs and dry grass, placed in the hollow spout of a dead limb, or (at Norfolk Island) in the trunk of a dead tree-fern, at varying heights from the ground. Some that I saw at Norfolk Island were within easy reach from the ground.'

Nest size: width 100 mm (4 in); height 150 mm (6 in)
Clutch size: *c.* 2–3
Collected: 21 December 1912, in a tree fern near the ground on Norfolk Island by Australian ornithologist Gregory M. Mathews
Conservation: Extinct

White-throated Dipper

Cinclus cinclus gularis

The five dipper species are the only songbirds whose entire life is spent in and around fast-flowing water. This White-throated Dipper nest is a typical example of their relatively large, spherical, lined nest with a side entrance. All the dippers, whether in the New World or the Old World, build similar, globular nests. The main structure is often of moss and the nests are always close to the stream or river where they live – sometimes even within it – with a few famous examples being found behind waterfalls in the early 1800s. The use of moss can be so successful in camouflaging the dome as part of the bank that they are often only found by watching the parents' return with food. Both sexes build the nests, sometimes using a cavity or bent fern as the main support onto which the overlaying lumps of moss is added. The female then gently lines it with dry leaves into which three white eggs are laid.

Nest size: overall nest size width 240 mm (9½ in); height 230 mm (9 in); depth 160 mm (6¼ in)
Clutch size: 3
Collected: nest – 17 June 1983, Denbighshire, Wales; eggs – 21 April 1939, Llandysul, Wales
Conservation: Least Concern

Cinclus cinclus.
Llangollen, Clwyd, 17/6/83
(had 3 eggs 7/6, empty on 17/6)
P J K Burton

Cinclus cinclus cinclus
Llangollen, Clwyd, Wales
17 June 1983
PJK Burton (B)

Black Redstart

Phoenicurus ochruros gibraltariensis

This Black Redstart nest and single egg, collected in Cambridge, England, is one of the first known examples of their nesting in the British Isles. The first definitive proof of breeding in the UK was in Sussex in 1923 and they first bred in Cambridge in 1937. The Black Redstart is unusual for a rare British breeding bird in that it often chooses to breed in built up urban areas. In the 1930s and 1940s, at the height of the Second World War, Black Redstarts nested repeatedly at several sites in the centre of Cambridge. In 1941 a pair nested on the roof of Christ's College, Cambridge and the following year a pair nested in a hole in the wall of the Chemistry Laboratories in Downing Street. This neat cup of grasses, moss, string, hair and feathers would have been built by both sexes but primarily by the female. Their nests are always placed in a suitably sheltered crevice, and they often build their nests in man-made features such as sheds or walls, even old swallows' nests. It was the wartime bombing of British cities that inadvertently created the ideal nesting habitat. In 1943 almost all the UK breeding pairs depended on bomb damage for their nesting sites and over 20 years later in 1964 it was estimated there were 16 pairs nesting in bombsites in Cheapside, London. By 1973 there was 63 breeding pairs recorded in the UK, but the latest data suggests breeding numbers may have decreased since the late 1970s.

Nest size: cup width 60 mm (2¼ in); 35 mm (1¼ in)
Clutch size: 4-6
Collected: *c.* late 1930s, Cambridge, England
by E. L. Arnold & D. J. Moltens
Conservation: Least Concern

White's Thrush

Zoothera aurea toratugumi

Thrushes and their relatives are some of our most familiar garden birds, for example, the American Robin is a thrush and one of the most numerous wild bird species in North America. However, White's Thrush is only found in the Far East, from Siberia to Korea and Japan. This large, beautifully constructed cup nest is typical of those built by thrushes. Most build cup nests made of grasses and other plant materials, and many use mud to bind them or line the nest. This example, built by the female, is made from mosses, twigs, grasses and rootlets which she has cemented together using mud. The cup has then been carefully lined with pine needles into which four light blue eggs, finely speckled with red have been laid. Deforestation and forest degradation are the biggest threats to this, the largest of the Japanese thrushes.

Nest size: cup width 100 mm (4 in); cup depth 50 mm (2 in)
Clutch size: 4
Collected: 1 June 1923, Subashiri near the base of Mount Fuji, Honshu, Japan by Y. Okada for Lieutenant Colonel Ronald F. Meiklejohn (1876–1949)
Conservation: Least Concern

Taxonomy

List of orders and families with Natural History Museum (NHM) reference number.

STRUTHIONIFORMES
STRUTHIONIDAE Ostriches
p.12 Syrian Ostrich *Struthio camelus syriacus*, E/1941.4.1.69

CASUARIIFORMES
CASUARIIDAE Cassowaries, Emus
p.14 Dwarf Cassowary *Casuarius bennetti*, E/1858.4.27.33-33.x

ANSERIFORMES
ANATIDAE Ducks, Geese & Swans
p.16 Emperor Goose *Anser canagicus*, NHMUK N/193.380
p.18 Green-winged Teal *Anas crecca*, NHMUK N/2015.2.24

GALLIFORMES
PHASIANIDAE Partridges, Pheasants and Grouse
p.20 Common Pheasant *Phasianus colchicus colchicus*, NHMUK N/2015.2.23.a

PODICIPEDIFORMES
PODICIPEDIDAE Grebes
p.22 Little Grebe *Tachybaptus ruficollis ruficollis*, NHMUK N/2015.2.3

COLUMBIFORMES
COLUMBIDAE Pigeons
p.24 White-capped Fruit-Dove *Ptilinopus dupetithouarsii dupetithouarsii*, NHMUK N/2016.3.1

EURYPYGIFORMES
EURYPYGIDAE Sunbittern
p.26 Sunbittern *Eurypyga helias helias*, NHMUK N/139.1

CAPRIMULGIFORMES
PODARGIDAE Frogmouths
p.28 Gould's Frogmouth *Batrachostomus stellatus*, NHMUK N/2003.3.1
p.30 Sri Lanka Frogmouth *Batrachostomus moniliger*, NHMUK E/1976.1.268

APODIDAE Swifts
p.32 Sabine's Spinetail *Rhaphidura sabini*, NHMUK N/180.6
p.34 White-nest Swiftlet *Aerodramus fuciphagus fuciphagus*, NHMUK N/78.1
TROCHILIDAE Hummingbirds
p.36 Juan Fernández Firecrown *Sephanoides fernandensis*, NHMUK N/247.15

CUCULIFORMES
CUCULIDAE Cuckoos
p.38 Common Cuckoo *Cuculus canorus canorus*, in Rock Pipit nest 1902.1.10.699 and eggs 1902.1.10.693-8

GRUIFORMES
RALLIDAE Rails, Coots
p.40 Laysan Rail *Zapornia palmeri*, NHMUK N/193.61

SPHENISCIFORMES
SPHENISCIDAE Penguins
p.42 Emperor Penguin *Aptenodytes forsteri*, NHMUK E/1916.9.8.1-3

PROCELLARIIFORMES
HYDROBATIDAE Northern Storm-Petrels
p.44 European Storm-Petrel *Hydrobates pelagicus*, NHMUK N/2021.10.2

PELECANIFORMES
SULIDAE Gannets, Boobies
p.46 Northern Gannet *Morus bassanus*, NHMUK N/1975.1.1

CHARADRIIFORMES
RECURVIROSTRIDAE Stilts, Avocets
p.48 Pied Avocet *Recurvirostra avosetta*, NHMUK N/1985.1.3
CHARADRIIDAE Plovers, Lapwings
p.50 Golden Plover *Pluvialis apricaria apricaria*, NHMUK N/2015.2.35
SCOLOPACIDAE Sandpipers
p.52 Red-necked Phalarope *Phalaropus lobatus*, NHMUK N/2021.10.1
ALCIDAE Auks
p.54 Great Auk *Pinguinus impennis*, BMNH E/1941.1.1.2
STERCORARIIDAE Skuas, Jaegers
p.56 Parasitic Jaeger *Stercorarius parasiticus*,

NHMUK N/2015.2.23.b
LARIDAE Gulls, Terns
p.58 Brown Noddy *Anous stolidus stolidus*, NHMUK N/199.1

ACCIPITRIFORMES
ACCIPITRIDAE Kites, Hawks and Eagles
p.60 Hen Harrier *Circus cyaneus cyaneus*, NHMUK N/2015.2.13

COLIIFORMES
COLIIDAE Mousebirds
p.62 Red-faced Mousebird *Urocolius indicus lacteifrons*, NHMUK N/2006.1.83

BUCEROTIFORMES
UPUPIDAE Hoopoes
p.64 Common Hoopoe *Upupa epops epops*, NHMUK N/203.29

PICIFORMES
PICIDAE Woodpeckers
p.66 Buff-spotted Woodpecker *Campethera nivosa nivosa*, NHMUK N/202.1
RAMPHASTIDAE Toucans, Barbets
p.68 Red-fronted Tinkerbird *Pogoniulus pusillus affinis*, NHMUK N/193.649

CORACIIFORMES
MEROPIDAE Bee-Eaters
p.70 Black-headed Bee-eater *Merops breweri*, E/1980.1.1

PSITTACIFORMES
PSITTACULIDAE Old World Parrots
p.72 Echo Parakeet *Psittacula eques echo*, NHMUK N/1990.1.1

PASSERIFORMES
PITTIDAE Pittas
p.74 Superb Pitta *Pitta superba*, NHMUK N/193.312
EURYLAIMIDAE Typical Broadbills
p.76 Dusky Broadbill *Corydon sumatranus*, NHMUK N/129.1
CALYPTOMENIDAE African and Green Broadbills
p.78 African Broadbill *Smithornis capensis*, NHMUK N/115.1
PIPRIDAE Manakins
p.80 Golden-headed Manakin *Ceratopipra*

erythrocephala erythrocephala, NHMUK N/267.24
COTINGIDAE Cotingas
p.82 Green-and-Black Fruiteater *Pipreola riefferii*, NHMUK N/56.33
PLATYRINCHIDAE Spadebills and Allies
p.84 White-throated Spadebill *Platyrinchus mystaceus*, NHMUK N/1976.6.1
PIPROMORPHIDAE Flatbills
p86 Slaty-capped Flycatcher *Leptopogon superciliaris superciliaris*, NHMUK N/50.1
TYRANNIDAE Tyrant Flycatchers
p.88 Scissor-tailed Flycatcher *Tyrannus forficatus*, NHMUK N/40.1
p.90 San Cristóbal Vermilion Flycatcher *Pyrocephalus rubinus dubius*, NHMUK N/2008.2.1
THAMNOPHILIDAE Antbirds
p.92 Great Antshrike *Taraba major semifasciatus*, NHMUK N/2020.5.4
FURNARIIDAE Horneros, Foliage-Gleaners and Spinetails
p.94 Rufous Hornero *Furnarius rufus*, NHMUK N/193.430
MENURIDAE Lyrebirds
p.96 Prince Albert's Lyrebird *Menura alberti*, Stub Record 1853.5.7.1 and 1853.5.7.2
PTILONORHYNCHIDAE Bowerbirds
p.98 Tooth-billed Bowerbird *Scenopoeetes dentirostris*, NHMUK N/193.389
MALURIDAE Fairywrens, Grasswrens
p.100 Southern Emu-Wren *Stipiturus malachurus westernensis*, NHMUK N/1975.5.1
MELIPHAGIDAE Honeyeaters
p.102 Sclater's Myzomela *Myzomela sclateri*, NHMUK N/241.1
ACANTHIZIDAE Thornbills and Allies
p.104 Yellow-rumped Thornbill *Acanthiza chrysorrhoa leighi*, NHMUK N/87.11
POMATOSTOMIDAE Australasian or Pseudo-Babblers
p.106 Grey-crowned Babbler *Pomatostomus temporalis temporalis*, NHMUK N/102.1
MELANOCHARITIDAE Berrypeckers and Longbills
p.108 Spectacled Longbill *Oedistoma iliolophus fergussonis*, NHMUK N/193.356
CALLAEIDAE Wattlebirds
p.110 South Island Saddleback/Tīeke *Philesturnus carunculatus*, NHMUK N/193.357
CAMPEPHAGIDAE Cuckooshrikes

p.112 Andaman Large Cuckooshrike *Coracina javensis andamana,* NHMUK N/82.2
CINCLOSOMATIDAE Quail-thrushes and Jewel-babblers
p.114 Spotted Quail-thrush *Cinclosoma punctatum dovei,* NHMUK N/163.1
PACHYCEPHALIDAE Whistlers and Allies
p.116 Rusty Pitohui *Pseudorectes ferrugineus ferrugineus,* NHMUK N/66.2
OREOICIDAE Australo-Papuan Bellbirds
p.118 Rufous-naped Bellbird *Aleadryas rufinucha niveifrons,* NHMUK N/264.14
VIREONIDAE Shrike Babblers, Erpornis and Vireos
p.120 Rufous-browed Peppershrike *Cyclarhis gujanensis flavipectus,* NHMUK N/193.83
ORIOLIDAE Old World Orioles
p.122 Stephen's Island/Takapourewa Piopio *Turnagra capensis minor,* NHMUK N/193.657
MACHAERIRHYNCHIDAE Boatbills
p.124 Black-breasted Boatbill *Machaerirhynchus nigripectus harterti,* NHMUK N/264.12
ARTAMIDAE Woodswallows, Australian Magpies and Allies
p.126 Gray Butcherbird *Cracticus torquatus cinereus,* NHMUK N/163.3
PLATYSTEIRIDAE Shrike-flycatchers, Wattle-Eyes and Batises
p.128 Boulton's Batis *Batis margaritae margaritae,* NHMUK N/2011.2.1
p.130 Banded Wattle-eye *Platysteira laticincta,* NHMUK N/2019.5.1
VANGIDAE Vangas, Helmetshrikes, and Allies
p.132 Madagascar Blue Vanga *Cyanolanius madagascarinus madagascarinus,* NHMUK N/193.482
AEGITHINIDAE Ioras
p.134 Common Iora *Aegithina tiphia horizoptera,* NHMUK N/193.111
MALACONOTIDAE Bushshrikes and Allies
p.136 Bokmakierie *Telophorus zeylonus zeylonus,* NHMUK N/112.2
DICRURIDAE Drongos
p.138 Aldabra Drongo *Dicrurus aldabranus,* NHMUK N/261.14
RHIPIDURIDAE Fantails
p.140 Long-tailed Fantail *Rhipidura opistherythra,* NHMUK N/193.239
LANIIDAE Shrikes
p.142 Masked Shrike *Lanius nubicus,* NHMUK N/30.1
CORVIDAE Crows, Jays, and Magpies
p.144 Rook *Corvus frugilegus frugilegus,* NHMUK N/2013.3.1
MONARCHIDAE Monarch Flycatchers
p.146 Marquesas Monarch *Pomarea mendozae motanensis,* NHMUK N/2019.9.2
CORCORACIDAE White-winged Chough and Apostlebird
p.148 White-winged Chough *Corcorax melanorhamphos melanoramphos,* NHMUK N/87.8
IFRITIDAE Ifrita
p.150 Blue-capped Ifrita *Ifrita kowaldi kowaldi,* NHMUK N/193.456
PARADISAEIDAE Birds-of-Paradise
p.152 Greater Bird-of-Paradise *Paradisaea apoda apoda,* NHMUK N/193.514
EUPETIDAE Rockfowl, Rockjumper and Rail-babbler
p.154 Gray-necked Rockfowl *Picathartes oreas,* NHMUK N/107.1
PETROICIDAE Australasian Robins
p.156 Flame Robin *Petroica phoenicea,* NHMUK N/163.5
DICAEIDAE Flowerpeckers
p.158 Orange-bellied Flowerpecker *Dicaeum trigonostigma cinereigulare,* NHMUK N/171.2
NECTARINIIDAE Sunbirds
p.160 Carmelite Sunbird *Chalcomitra fuliginosa aurea,* NHMUK N/2006.1.38
PRUNELLIDAE Accentors
p.162 Dunnock *Prunella modularis modularis,* NHMUK N/193.108
PLOCEIDAE Weavers
p.164 Village Weaver *Ploceus cucullatus cucullatus,* NHMUK N/178.1
p.166 Ibadan Malimbe *Malimbus ibadanensis,* NHMUK N/253.1
PASSERIDAE Sparrows, Snowfinches and Allies
p.168 House Sparrow *Passer domesticus biblicus,* NHMUK N/2023.9.1
MOTACILLIDAE Wagtails, Pipits
p.170 Cape Wagtail *Motacilla capensis capensis,* NHMUK N/117.2
FRINGILLIDAE Finches, Euphonias and Hawaiian Honeycreepers
p.172 Maui 'Alauahio *Paroreomyza montana,* NHMUK N/1997.26.2
PLECTROPHENACIDAE Longspurs, Snow Buntings

p.174 Snow Bunting *Plectrophenax nivalis nivalis*, NHMUK N/35.3

PASSERELLIDAE New World Sparrows and Allies

p.176 White-naped Brushfinch *Atlapetes albinucha gutturalis*, NHMUK N/56.1

EMBERIZIDAE Old World Buntings

p.178 Black-headed Bunting *Granativora melanocephala*, NHMUK N/239.5

PHAENICOPHILIDAE Warbler Tanagers

p.180 Jamaican Spindalis *Spindalis nigricephala*, NHMUK N/248.1

ICTERIDAE New World Blackbirds

p.182 Streak-backed Oriole *Icterus pustulatus sclateri*, NHMUK N/53.1

CARDINALIDAE Cardinals, Grosbeaks and Allies

p.184 Painted Bunting *Passerina ciris ciris*, NHMUK N/193.99

THRAUPIDAE Tanagers

p.186 Large Cactus Finch *Geospiza conirostris propinqua*, NHMUK N/2008.2.20

STENOSTIRIDAE Fairy Flycatchers, Crested-Flycatchers

p.188 White-tailed Crested-Flycatcher *Elminia albonotata subcaerulea*, NHMUK N/190.4

PARIDAE Tits, Chickadees

p.190 Blue Tit *Cyanistes caeruleus obscurus*, NHMUK N/2023.4.1

REMIZIDAE Penduline Tits

p.192 Cape Penduline Tit *Anthoscopus minutus damarensis*, NHMUK N/2006.1.82

ALAUDIDAE Larks

p.194 Liben Lark *Heteromirafra archeri sidamoensis*, NHMUK N/2018.2.1

PANURIDAE Bearded Reedling

p.196 Bearded Reedling *Panurus biarmicus biarmicus*, NHMUK N/193.328

MACROSPHENIDAE Crombecs, Longbills and Allies

p.198 Long-billed Crombec S*ylvietta rufescens ansorgei*, NHMUK N/2006.1.80

CISTICOLIDAE Cisticolas

p.200 Desert Cisticola *Cisticola aridulus kalahari*, NHMUK N/189.96

LOCUSTELLIDAE Bush Warblers

p.202 Rusty Thicketbird *Megalurulus rubiginosus*, NHMUK N/193.410

ACROCEPHALIDAE Brush, Reed and Swamp Warblers

p.204 Laysan Millerbird *Acrocephalus familiaris familiaris*, NHMUK N/193.60

HIRUNDINIDAE Swallows

p.206 Welcome Swallow *Hirundo neoxena neoxena*, NHMUK N/105.1

PYCNONOTIDAE Bulbuls

p.208 Styan's or Taiwanese light-vented Bulbul *Pycnonotus taivanus formosae*, NHMUK N/2021.14.2

PHYLLOSCOPIDAE Old World Leaf Warblers

p.210 Gray-cheeked Leaf Warbler *Seicercus poliogenys*, NHMUK N/219.1153

SCOTOCERCIDAE Brush Warblers and Allies

p.212 Rufous-faced Warbler *Abroscopus albogularis fulvifacies*, NHMUK N/164.12 and NHMUK N/164.3

AEGITHALIDAE Long-Tailed Tits

p.214 Long-tailed Tit *Aegithalos caudatus trivirgatus*, NHMUK N/193.675

SYLVIIDAE Sylvia Warblers, Parrotbills and Allies

p.216 Eurasian Blackcap *Sylvia atricapilla atricapilla*, NHMUK N/1.1

ZOSTEROPIDAE White-Eyes

p.218 Golden White-eye *Cleptornis marchei*, NHMUK N/193.42 and NHMUK E/1961.4.3

TIMALIIDAE Scimitar Babblers and Allies

p.220 Golden Babbler *Cyanoderma chrysaeum chrysaeum*, NHMUK N/219.1203

PELLORNEIDAE Smaller Babblers

p.222 Scaly-breasted Illadopsis *Illadopsis albipectus*, NHMUK N/2002.2.2 and NHMUK E/2014.1.1

LEIOTHRICHIDAE Babblers, Laughing-Thrushes and Allies

p.224 Red-billed Leiothrix *Leiothrix lutea calipyga*

REGULIDAE Goldcrests, Kinglets

p.216 Madeira Firecrest *Regulus madeirensis*, NHMUK N/193.258, stub record E/1941.1.6.148

BOMBYCILLIDAE Waxwings

p.228 Bohemian Waxwing *Bombycilla garrulus garrulus*, NHMUK N/22.7

HYPOCOLIIDAE Hypocolius

p.230 Hypocolius *Hypocolius ampelinus*, NHMUK N/188.4, stub record E/1922.12.20.29

CERTHIIDAE Treecreepers

p.232 Sikkim Treecreeper *Certhia discolor*, NHMUK N/219.12

SITTIDAE Nuthatches, Spotted Creepers and Wallcreeper

p.234 Corsican Nuthatch *Sitta whiteheadi*, NHMUK N/28.1and stub record 1884.7.16.55-57

TROGLODYTIDAE Wrens

p.236 Marsh Wren *Cistothorus palustris
palustris,* NHMUK N/36.6
POLIOPTILIDAE Gnatcatchers
p.238 Blue-gray Gnatcatcher *Polioptila caerulea
caerulea,* NHMUK N/193.105
MIMIDAE Mockingbirds, Thrashers
p.240 San Cristóbal Mockingbird *Mimus
melanotis,* NHMUK N/193.198 and
E/1941.2.5.22
STURNIDAE Starlings
p.242 Norfolk Starling *Aplonis fusca fusca,*
NHMUK N/193.511 and NHMUK E/1941.2.1.200
CINCLIDAE Dippers
p.244 White-throated Dipper *Cinclus cinclus
gularis,* NHMUK N/2019.2.1
MUSCICAPIDAE Chats, Flycatchers
p.246 Black Redstart *Phoenicurus ochruros
gibraltariensis,* NHMUK N/13.1 and stub record
E/1973.21.2
TURDIDAE Thrushes
p.248 White's Thrush *Zoothera aurea
toratugum*i, NHMUK N/193.377

Nest of Bokmaklerle, *Telophorus
zeylonus zeylonus* (see p.136)

First published by the Natural History Museum, Cromwell Road, London SW7 5BD
© The Trustees of the Natural History Museum, London 2024

Photography by Jonathan Jackson.

ISBN 978 0 565 09552 9

A catalogue record for this book is available from the British Library.

10 9 8 7 6 5 4 3 2 1

Reproduction by Saxon Digital Services, UK
Printed by Toppan Leefung Printing Ltd, China